ISBN 978-1-331-20882-2
PIBN 10158623

1 MONTH OF
FREE
READING

at
www.ForgottenBooks.com

By purchasing this book you are eligible for one month membership to ForgottenBooks.com, giving you unlimited access to our entire collection of over 1,000,000 titles via our web site and mobile apps.

To claim your free month visit: www.forgottenbooks.com/free158623

English
Français
Deutsche
Italiano
Español
Português

www.forgottenbooks.com

Mythology Photography **Fiction**
Fishing Christianity **Art** Cooking
Essays Buddhism Freemasonry
Medicine **Biology** Music **Ancient
Egypt** Evolution Carpentry Physics
Dance Geology **Mathematics** Fitness
Shakespeare **Folklore** Yoga Marketing
Confidence Immortality Biographies
Poetry **Psychology** Witchcraft
Electronics Chemistry History **Law**
Accounting **Philosophy** Anthropology
Alchemy Drama Quantum Mechanics
Atheism Sexual Health **Ancient History**
Entrepreneurship Languages Sport
Paleontology Needlework Islam
Metaphysics Investment Archaeology
Parenting Statistics Criminology
Motivational

TACKLING TECH.

Suggestions for the Undergraduate in Technical School or College

By

LAWRENCE WICKES CONANT

NEW YORK

THE RONALD PRESS COMPANY

1922

To the Memory of

DR. RICHARD COCKBURN MACLAURIN

Whose self-sacrificing service brought
into being "New Technology"

FOREWORD

Life ordinarily is, and should be, an educational process from first to last. Experience begins in the very earliest days of life, and continues throughout all its stages. The earlier years may be termed the "formative period," and it is certainly important that during this period proper guidance and the inculcation of wise habits and principles should be the foremost consideration. It is well, then, that the experience of those who have traversed the road should be made available for those who are just beginning the journey. Everyone who has had the opportunity of college training must certainly realize that his course would have been more effective and satisfactory had there been available to him the best and wisest advice beforehand. From this it follows that any method or medium which can present to the undergraduate student intelligibly and in an interesting fashion for utilization such experience as comes from men who have been closely and recently in touch with the personal problems which he will have to face, cannot fail to be of great value and assistance.

The book to which I am pleased to contribute this foreword is the outcome of careful analysis

and discussion, by the author, of the several subjects considered in its sixteen chapters, and it
embodies, for the benefit of students and their ad-
visers, much valuable information in a convenient
form.   It emphasizes very strongly the things
the undergraduate will need in his course of training as a preparation for his later life, professional
or otherwise, and at the same time brings strongly
before him the fact that his college life and work
are indeed a very important part of his whole
life itself.   It encourages him to apply to his
problems systematic work and gives him valuable counsel as to the relations of the different
activities, social and otherwise, in which he may
share along with his professional or technical
training.

What measure of success the author and those
who have assisted him may achieve in the task
they have set before them will, it is hoped, prove
that the effort has been worth while.

ELIHU THOMSON

Lynn, Massachusetts,
    September 1, 1922.

AUTHOR'S NOTE

The suggestions here presented, the outgrowth originally of the author's personal experience as an undergraduate, have been checked and broadened by the criticism of men in responsible touch with student life in a number of institutions. While a few of the topics discussed, such as "Summer Work, Getting a Job and Making Good," apply more definitely to students in the later years of college or technical school, most of the chapters will be found useful throughout the undergraduate course, and for high school students preparing to enter college or a technical school. This is the case, for example, with "Preparing for a Technical Education," the chapter on "Health and Energy," and those on "Personal Finance."

The author is deeply sensible of the kindness of the busy men who have taken time for personal consideration of this discussion of undergraduate problems. He is under peculiar obligation to the officers and teachers of the Massachusetts Institute of Technology for their continued encouragement and assistance, particularly Dr. Elihu Thomson, Acting President; Dr. Davis R. Dewey, head of the Department of Engineering Administration; Professor H. G. Pearson, head of the Department of English; and Professor Erwin H. Schell, head of the Department of Economics, who is responsible, indeed, for the first conception of the book.

Acknowledgment should be made also to the deans and other representatives of other educational institutions—especially to Colonel Edward K. Strong, Jr., and Messrs. C. M. Nichols and C. C. Crawford, of the Carnegie Institute of Technology; Professor Richard Wellington Husband, Associate Dean of Dartmouth College; Dean Raymond Walters of Swarthmore College; and Dean L. P. Mitchell of the Engineering College of Syracuse University.

LAWRENCE WICKES CONANT

Cambridge, Massachusetts,
September 1, 1922.

CONTENTS

CONTENTS

LIST OF ILLUSTRATIONS

TACKLING TECH.

CHAPTER I

PREPARING FOR A TECHNICAL EDUCATION

The Hills have been steep for man's mounting,
The Woods have been dense for his axe,
The Stars have been thick for his counting,
The Sands have been wide for his tracks,
The Sea has been deep for his diving,
The Poles have been broad for his sway,
But bravely he's proved by his striving
That where there's a will 'there's a way.

—The Open Window

Minimum Preparation Required

The minimum amount of preparation required for entrance into any technical institution is usually a high school education. You must first complete satisfactorily this preliminary training before you will be allowed to enter the higher institution without conditions. How careful should you be to fulfil this requirement, and how far is it wise for you to go in exceeding it?

If you enter a technical school burdened with one or more conditions you give yourself a poor start. Where there is absolutely no alternative, this handicap must, of course, be borne. If this is the case, the best policy is not to worry. Some

3

conditions are signed off automatically by passing the subjects which follow them; the others can usually be taken care of within two years after entering without carrying a serious overload. Thirty or forty hours of work during a term will remove an ordinary condition. Before you plan to enter a technical institution under such circumstances, however, make sure that you have exhausted every alternative. *The man who enters with any conditions is poorly prepared.*

Exceeding the Requirements

It cannot be emphasized too strongly that in every possible way you should strive not only to meet, but to *exceed* the requirements for admission. This may be done in two ways: first, by obtaining a mark beyond question in every subject required for admission; and second, by studying and passing a number of additional subjects of a general nature. Begin carrying out these two policies from the moment you decide upon the college or the technical school that you are to enter.

To cite an instance, I will mention a fellow whom I knew in high school and who very early planned to get a technical education. He was able to obtain most of the preparation required during his four high school years, although it involved two years of outside tutoring in French. Throughout this time he made it a rule to take additional subjects, such as Ancient History and Advanced Elocution. Later he found that much of this training and experience was valuable. The policy of going the "uncompelled mile" in the matter of preparation is a wise one to follow.

Advantages of Additional Preparation

Frequently a man who thinks himself ready to begin his technical education immediately will do well to prepare himself still further. There are two ways of doing this: first, by attending a preparatory school for an additional year; and second, by entering college. The reason why men usually hesitate about taking either of these courses is that they feel it will mean too great an additional investment of time or money. The idea of an extra year of study looks appalling to a young fellow who already feels "old" at eighteen or nineteen.

If barely sufficient money is available to put a man through a four years' course, very few parents would consider allowing him to take a preliminary year at a preparatory school, if that would make it necessary to borrow a thousand dollars for his last year in college. Yet that one additional year might easily enable the man to double the benefits which he might get from his course of training. There is no point where an added investment has a more telling effect than in the field of fullest preparation. To be "penny wise" here, either in the matter of time or money, is indeed to be "pound foolish" as regards your entire investment in an education.

Let me cite one instance of the way in which this works out in practice. I recall the case of a friend who had carefully prepared throughout his high school course to enter a certain engineering school. By the time he had obtained his high school diploma he had practically covered the requirements for the institution he wished to enter. Nevertheless, he felt that further preparation would strengthen his preliminary training. Accordingly he entered a preparatory school for a year. Here he derived benefits which were of greatest value. He learned *how* to study; he was initiated into various student activities; he widened tremendously his circle of friends and increased his ability to make new ones. When finally he entered the technical school he had a running start on the men who came directly from high school. Hundreds of others have had similar experiences. The year of additional preparation is usually worth all it costs.

College Preparation for a Technical Education

At present the proportion of college transfers in many technical institutions is increasing. It is not to be supposed from this that our technical schools are sooner or later to become mere graduate institutions. The requirements for entrance have been changed little, if any. In practically every case they can be met satisfactorily by the graduate of a good high school. There are, in fact, several arguments in favor of a man's not waiting too long before beginning the more rigorous technical training.

The shock of coming direct from high school to the technical institution is not likely to be very much more severe than that of coming from high school to college. The amount of work required in the scientific school eliminates many of the dangers which beset the college man, for the technical student has little time for mischief. At the same time the difficulty of the work should not be exaggerated, and the technical education should hold no terrors for the student of reasonable maturity and mental capacity.

College Men in Technical Schools

While all this is true and while the necessity for a breadth of training is recognized in many scientific schools, the combination of both a college and a technical education has in many cases distinct advantages. So many are at present following this method of education that it is interesting to note into what classes these men can be divided.

The college men attending technical institutions fall into four groups. First, there is the man whose mind was not made up at the time he went to college regarding what he wished to do in life, and who took this method to decide. Second, there is the man who wished to get a taste of college life, before getting down to the more serious job of studying for a profession. Third, there is the individual to whom the added time and money necessary meant no great sacrifice and who wished to obtain as varied an education as possible. Finally, there is the more mature college graduate, who has definitely chosen his goal in life and who feels the need of specialization in some technical field as a means to an end.

What College Preparation Is Best

In case a man has decided to take two years or more in college before entering a technical school, there is the question of what sort of college training he had best obtain. It is conceded quite generally that if he is later to specialize, his training in college may well be broad. Emphasis should probably be laid upon advanced courses in English, Literature, Economics, and History. He should, however, lay out a definite plan of action to cover the entire five or six years. In this should be included many of the general scientific studies which are required by the technical school before graduation and for which credit can later be obtained. Added to these should be a thorough preparation in Mathematics, Physics, and Chemistry, since these subjects can often be covered to better advantage in college than elsewhere. Correspondence, or, if possible, consultation with the officers of the technical school when the college student first begins to map out his course is of the greatest benefit in obtaining satisfactory results.

For example, a man who had taken two years in college, and with whom I became acquainted at Technology, had followed out this method successfully. He had studied German, French, and Spanish, as well as the sciences of Biology, Chemistry, and Physics. The training received from such courses in college broadens one's outlook. It develops a deeper appreciation of the "other things" to be found in life than can usually be obtained in even the most liberal of technical courses.

Later Advantages of College Preparation

The advantages of previous college training which develop after a man has entered the technical school may well be pointed out more specifically. In the first place, he has a sufficient background of knowledge and experience to know what he wants to get at the technical school. Next, he has a clearer perception of the relative importance of technical and general studies, as well as of other activities open to him. Finally, his more mature and better developed mind enables him to get what he wants with comparative ease.

I recall a case which brings out these points, that of a friend who came to the Massachusetts Institute of Technology after he had completed an A. B. course at Yale. His four years in college had enabled him to map out a definite plan of action, not only for his technical training, but for life. When many of his classmates were struggling to maintain the pace set by the instructors, this man was only moderately busy. He seemed to have plenty of time to do his studies better than anyone else, yet he was able also to have considerable leisure and to enjoy life to the fullest extent.

When such a man graduates from a technical school he takes with him not his degree alone, but also a well-rounded professional training that will soon enable him to command some very substantial returns on the added money and time that he has invested. His policy has been a wise one. He is likely to keep a lap ahead of the other runners in the race.

Experience and Maturity Through Work

Not infrequently it happens that, as regards his studies, a man may be prepared for a technical education beyond all question, but may still lack a certain degree of maturity which is very desirable. The principles dealt with in the specialized training of technical schools can be grasped more readily by the matured mind. Physical age is of considerable importance, for many technical institutions do not allow students to enter below the age of seventeen, and others recommend the ages of eighteen or nineteen as being more desirable.

When the question of age and maturity has to be carefully weighed, and when financial considerations prevent taking an extra year in preparatory school or college, work in some industry for a year offers an excellent alternative. If suitable employment is found the experience to be gained is of the greatest value.[1] Parents or students troubled by the problem of deciding

[1] See Chapter XV.

TECHNICAL COURSES OFFERED

Name of School	Location	No. of Students 1920-21	Entrance by	Resident Tuition	Non-Resident Tuition	Technical Courses Offered (best reading)
Alabama Poly. Ins.	Auburn, Ala.	1195	C or E	$25	$61	Physics, Metallurgy, Mechanical Eng., Mathematics, Electrical Eng., Economics, Civil Eng., Chemical Eng., Chemistry, Biology, Architectural Eng., Architecture, Agricultural Eng.
Armour Inst. of Tech.	Chicago, Ill.	2280	C or E	200	200	Physics, Mechanical Eng., Mathematics, Electrical Eng., General Eng., Civil Eng., Chemical Eng., Architecture
Calif. Inst. of Tech.	Pasadena, Calif.	395	C or E	200	200	Physical Chemistry, Physics, Mechanical Eng., Mathematics, Electrical Eng., Economics, Civil Eng., Chemical Eng., Chemistry, Biology, Aeronautical Eng.
Calif., Univ. of.	Berkeley, Calif.	1462	C or E	50	150	Sanitary Eng., Physical Chemistry, Physics, Mining Eng., Metallurgy, Mechanical Eng., Mathematics, Geology, Electrical Eng., Civil Eng., Chemical Eng., Chemistry, Biology, Architectural Eng., Architecture, Naval Architecture, Agricultural Eng.
Carnegie Inst. of Th.	Pittsburgh, Pa.	4982	C or E	200	200	Physics, Mining Eng., Metallurgy, Mechanical Eng., Mathematics, Electrical Eng., Civil Eng., Chemical Eng., Chemistry, Architecture
Case Sch. of Applied Science	Cleveland, Ohio	786	C or E	200	200	Physics, Mining Eng., Mechanical Eng., Mathematics, Geology, Electrical Eng., Civil Eng., Chemical Eng., Chemistry, Biology
Colo., Univ. of.	Boulder, Colo.	3254	C or E	45	90	Sanitary Eng., Physics, Mining Eng., Metallurgy, Mechanical Eng., Mathematics, Geology, Electrical Eng., Economics, Civil Eng., Chemical Eng., Chemistry, Biology, Architecture, Agricultural Eng.
Columbia Univ. of	New York, N.Y.	26658	C or E	345	345	Textile Eng., Sanitary Eng., Physical Chemistry, Physics, Metallurgy, Mechanical Eng., Mathematics, Industrial Eng., General Eng., Geology, Electrical Eng., Economics, Commercial Eng., Civil Eng., Chemical Eng., Chemistry, Biology and Public Health, Biology, Naval Architecture, Architecture, Administrative Eng.
Cornell Univ.	Ithaca, N.Y.	5718	C or E	250	250	Physics, Mining Eng., Mechanical Eng., Mathematics, Marine Eng., Geology, Electrical Eng., Economics, Civil Eng., Chemical Eng., Chemistry, Architecture, Agricultural Eng.
Drexel Inst.	Phila., Pa.	2646	C or E	195	195	Mechanical Eng., Mathematics, Electrical Eng., Economics, Civil Eng., Chemistry, Architecture
Ga. Sch. of Tech.	Atlanta, Ga.	2634	C or E	100	175	Sanitary Eng., Physics, Metallurgy, Mechanical Eng., Mathematics, Geology, Electrical Eng., Economics, Civil Eng., Chemistry, Ceramic Eng., Architecture, Agricultural Eng.
George Washington Univ.	Washington, D.C.	2968	C or E	180	180	Sanitary Eng., Physics, Mechanical Eng., Mathematics, General Eng., Electrical Eng., Civil Eng., Chemistry, Administrative Eng.
Harvard Univ.	Cambridge, Mass.	5273	E	250	250	Sanitary Eng., Physical Chemistry, Physics, Mining Eng., Metallurgy, Mechanical Eng., Mathematics, Marine Eng., Industrial Eng., Geology, Electrochemical Eng., Electrical Eng., Economics, Civil Eng., Chemistry, Ceramic Eng., Biology and Public Health, Biology, Architectural Eng., Architecture
Illinois, Univ. of.	Urbana, Ill.	9493	C or E	0	75	Sanitary Eng., Physical Chemistry, Physics, Mining Eng., Metallurgy, Mechanical Eng., Mathematics, Geology, Electrical Eng., Economics, Civil Eng., Chemical Eng., Chemistry, Ceramic Eng., Biology, Architectural Eng., Architecture, Agricultural Eng.
Iowa State College.	Ames, Iowa.	6378	C or E	0	51	Physics, Mining Eng., Mechanical Eng., Mathematics, Geology, Electrical Eng., Economics, Civil Eng., Chemistry, Ceramic Eng., Biology, Agricultural Eng.
Lehigh University.	Bethlehem, Pa.	1104	C	300	300	Physics, Metallurgy, Mathematics, Marine Eng., Geology, Electrical Eng., Civil Eng., Chemical Eng., Chemistry
Lewis Institute.	Chicago, Ill.	1710	C	110	110	Mechanical Eng., Mathematics, Electrical Eng., Civil Eng., Chemistry
Johns Hopkins Univ.	Baltimore, Md.	3200	C or E	250	250	Physics, Metallurgy, Mechanical Eng., Mathematics, Geology, Electrical Eng., Economics, Civil Eng., Chemistry, Biology, Architecture, Administrative Eng.
Maine, University of.	Orono, Me.	1313	C or E	125	195	Physics, Mining Eng., Metallurgy, Mechanical Eng., Mathematics, Marine Eng., Geology, Electrical Eng., Economics, Civil Eng., Chemistry, Biology, Architectural Eng., Agricultural Eng.
Mass. Inst. of Tech.	Cambridge, Mass.	3535	E	300	300	Textile Eng., Sanitary Eng., Physical Chemistry, Physics, Mining Eng., Metallurgy, Mechanical Eng., Mathematics, Marine Eng., Industrial Eng., General Eng., Geological Eng., Geology, Electrochemical Eng., Electrical Eng., Economics, Civil Eng., Chemical Eng., Chemistry, Naval Architecture, Architecture, Aeronautical Eng., Administrative Eng.

Institution	Location		C or E		
Michigan Agri. Col.	E. Lansing, Mich.	2036	C or E	0	45
Mich. Col. of Mines	Houghton, Mich.	269	C or E	25	150
Michigan, Univ. of	Ann Arbor, Mich.	9401	C or E	97	122
Minnesota, Univ. of	Minneapolis, Minn.	8120	C or E	90	120
New Hampshire Col.	Durham, N.H.	818	C or E	279	75
New York Univ.	New York, N.Y.	*359	C or E	240	240
Northwestern Univ.	Evanston, Ill.	7759	C or E	200	200
Ohio State Univ.	Columbus, Ohio	7210	C or E	0	D0
Penn. State Col.	State College, Pa.	2936	C or E	0	...
Polytechnic Inst. Brooklyn	Brooklyn, N.Y.	1292	C or E	250	250
Princeton Univ.	Princeton, N.J.	1850	E	300	300
Purdue University	Lafayette, Ind.	2925	C or E	0	35
Rensselaer Poly. Inst.	Troy, N.Y.	1017	C or E	250	250
Rhode Island St. Col.	Kingston, R.I.	343	C or E	260	260
Rice Inst.	Houston, Texas	763	C or E	0	50
Rose Poly. Inst.	Terre Haute, Ind.	241	C or E	0	0
Sheffield Sc. Sch.	New Haven, Conn.	*378	C or E	300	300
Stanford Univ.	Cal.	2940	C or E	255	255
Stevens Inst. of Tech.	Hoboken, N.J.	780	C or E	275	275
Swarthmore College	Swarthmore, Pa.	507	C or E	250	250
Syracuse University	Syracuse, N.Y.	4854	C or E	275	275
Thayer Sch. of Civil Eng.**	Hanover, N.H.	1775	E	250	250
Tufts Col. Eng. Sch.	Medford, Mass.	406	C or E	250	250
Vermont, Univ. of	Burlington, Vt.	864	C or E	175	175
Virginia Poly. Inst.	Blacksburg, Va.	485	C or E	...	80
Virginia, Univ. of	Charlottesville, Va.	1639	E	85	160
Washington, Univ. of	Seattle, Wash.	7870	C or E	60	200
Wisconsin, Univ. of	Madison, Wis.	7294	C or E	...	124
Worcester Poly. Inst.	Worcester, Mass.	571	C or E	200	200

*Number of students in Engineering school only.
**Dartmouth College.

13

upon the best preparation for a technical education may do well in many cases to consider such work as a possibility

BIBLIOGRAPHY

Baker, R. P. Engineering Education.

Bishop, F. L. Engineering Education. (United States Bureau of Education.)

Humphreys, Dr. A. C. The College Graduate as an Engineer.

Iowa State College of Agriculture and Mechanic Arts. Education in Engineering.

McDaniel, A. B. Co-ordination in Engineering Instruction. (University of Illinois.)

Magnusson, C. E. The College Trained Engineer. (Journal of the American Institute of Electrical Engineers. Vol. 40, Sept. 1921, p. 730-36.)

Mann, C. R. A Study of Engineering Education.

National Society for the Promotion of Engineering Education. Proceedings.

Roe, J. W. College Training for Executives. (Industrial Management. Vol. 58, Dec. 1919, p. 458-61.)

Scott, Prof. A. C. College Training of Electrical Engineers.

University of Texas. Correlation of High School and College Courses in the Sciences.

Waddell and Harrington. Addresses to Engineering Students. (Kansas City, Missouri.)

CHAPTER II

HOW TO PLAN YOUR TIME AND DO YOUR WORK

. . If you can fill the unforgiving minute
With sixty seconds' worth of distance run
Yours is the Earth and everything that's in it,
And—which is more—you'll be a Man, my son!

—"IF," BY RUDYARD KIPLING

Meeting New Conditions

In prep school you found a good deal of pressure brought upon you to get your work done. In the technical school it is different. The opportunity to win is laid before you. The winning is up to you. You must run under your own power and the sooner your clutch is in, the better. This means initiative.

Forget what people have told you about the difficulties of a technical education. After you have struck your pace you will find that you can instinctively accelerate your step, although you must strive unremittingly. To accomplish this you must plan your own work and then hold yourself responsible for getting it done. Formerly you did not need to plan your work more than a day or two in advance. Now you must plan by the week.

15

Developing a Plan

Here is a bit of my own experience. At prep school I began like everyone else to do my work in a hit-or-miss fashion, but one day a teacher set me thinking. He said, "You fellows think you are very busy, but the trouble is you don't plan your work. We had a lad here once who carefully planned everything. He gave to his studies the time they deserved. He spent more time than most of you do on athletics and outside work. Still he was able to read considerably and he always had time for fun on the side." This so appealed to me that I was eager to try it. Although I did not realize it, here was "scientific management" applied to prep school.

I did try this method and by the time I graduated from prep school I had developed a fair but crude schedule. When I began my technical course, I tried various schemes. Ultimately they were all refined by trial and error until I reached a final plan which worked. I shall give you here a general but practicable scheme for planning your work. Its principles are sound and it has been proved efficient in practice, not by myself alone, but by many other graduates and undergraduates of technical institutions. It is easy to plan your work when you know how to go about it.

Co-operation with Instructors

Do not wait until too late to discover that if you will give them opportunity, your instructors stand ready to help you in every phase of planning your work and getting it done. Too many fellows feel that faculty members are unquestionably on the "other side of the fence," and consequently make few attempts to obtain from them any personal advice or assistance. In reality, most of the "Profs." have "been there themselves" and if approached properly will not only prove to be firm friends, but will also be of the greatest assistance in helping to solve the personal as well as the scholastic problems of school life.

Necessary Information and Materials

The first thing to do in laying out a schedule is to study the work you have to do. You can't tell when you should study for a chemistry recitation, for example, until you get a general idea of the work. But don't spend a week getting this preliminary information. Take special notes on these points in the first classes of the term. You are then ready to make out your preliminary schedule.

Next get a suitable schedule form. You have probably been furnished with printed program

	MON.	TUES.	WED.	THURS.	FRI.	SAT.
7-8	Math.	Physics	Math.	Physics	Math.	Math.
8-9	Break.	Break.	Break.	Break.	Break.	Break.
9-10	Math. 2-146	Ph. Chi.	Math. 2-146	Ph. Chi.	Math. 2-146	Phy. Lab.
10-11	Chem. 6-106	Mil. Sci. 3-370	Physics Lect. 10-250	Math.	Chem.	Mil. Sci. 3-370
11-12	Chem. Lab. 4-251	Draw. 2-335	Eng. Hist.	Draw. 2-335	Chem. 6-106	Phy. Lab. 4-441
12-1	Chem. Lab. 4-251	Draw. 2-335	Chem. Lect. 10-250	Draw. 2-335	Chem. Lect. 10-250	Phy. Lab. 4-441
1-2	Lunch	Lunch	Lunch	Lunch	Lunch	Lunch
2-3	Eng. Hist. 2-181	Physics 2-143	Eng. Hist. 2-181	Physics 2-143	Hist. Lect. 8-330	
3-4	Draw. 2-290	Gymnasium Phy. Traing	Chem. Lab. 4-251	Mil. Sci. 3-370	Gymnasium Phy. Traing	
4-5	Draw. 2-290	Read.	Chem. Lab. 4-251	Read.	Read.	
5-6	Activ.	Activ.	Activ.	Activ.	Activ.	
6-7	Dinner	Dinner	Dinner	Dinner	Dinner	
7-8	Frat.	Math.	←	Phy. Lab.	Chem.	
8-9	Frat.	Hist. Lect.	Movies	Chem.	Chem.	
9-10		Writing, etc.	→	Writing, etc.	Writing, etc.	
10-11	Read.	Eng. Hist.		Eng. Hist.	Eng. Hist.	
11-12						

Figure 1.   (a) Schedule Card (face)

cards on which you have filled in your classes only. You will need a more general form, covering all your working hours. Draw up a Schedule Card, similar in form and arrangement to the sample schedule card shown on page 18 (Figure 1 a).

The school has provided its own schedule, but not yours. Follow the example thus set and put your plan in writing. This will make it definite, and will have the additional advantage of avoiding much repetition and waste of time in the long run.

Taking Time to Plan

Take time *today* to plan your work. The directions below tell you explicitly how to go about it. If you do not know how to build a schedule, follow these directions carefully. If you have your own method which you think is good enough, follow it with equal care. The way recommended here is the result of four years of experience by many different men. Even though your own method may be better for your particular purposes, by trying this other way once you are likely to get some suggestions for improving yours. Be sure to read as far as the section on "Making Your Plan Work" before you begin to fill in your card.

Building a Schedule

The first step in making out a schedule is to decide points in regard to sleeping, eating, etc. Count on getting plenty of sleep.[1] If you can study an hour before breakfast, or with merely a bite to eat, get up at 7 and go to bed at 11. At first you may feel that you cannot do this to advantage, but a month's trial may surprise you, with excellent results. In this case, 3 hours will be your maximum amount of study time for any night. If you find by actual test that you cannot study to advantage in the morning, get up at 8 and go to bed at 12. You then must count on a maximum of 4 hours of study a night.[2]

Each day allow an hour for getting dressed and for breakfast. Allow an hour for lunch, and an hour to an hour and one-half for dinner. Plan to stop work Saturday at 1, and to begin again Monday morning. You need recreation in order to do your best work, and the week-end is the best opportunity for this. The man who can work all the time doesn't exist.

Plan definitely to make use of the time you have available between classes. For certain kinds of work these hours are most valuable. For any kind of work they are far more valuable

[1] See Chapter VII.
[2] See Chapter III.

than no time at all. Count on filling them in, and soon you will learn to utilize them fully.

The next step in planning your work is to analyze, first, the work you have to do, and then the time you have to do it in. The schedule card will help you do this. This step will require but little effort and will give you an excellent idea of where your time actually goes. Be sure to read entirely through the chapter before putting anything down on your card. Then return to this point and *follow the directions carefully.*

Analyzing Your Work and Time

Draw up a blank schedule card similar to the sample shown in Figure 1 a and b (pages 18 and 22), and fill it out as follows. Make your entries in pencil. *This schedule is not to be copied. Use it as a sample and make out one of your own. Learn how to plan your own work.*

1. In the oblong spaces of your schedule card write in the name (or number) of each class which you have, showing also room numbers, etc., as on the sample schedule. In column (I) on the back of the card (see Figure 1 b) fill in the number of hours for classes for each day and the total for the week.

2. In the small squares show, by means of vertical lines, the number of hours of preparation

	I CLASS HOURS	II PREPARATION HOURS
M		
T		
W		
Th		
F		
S	_____	_____
Total		
Total Hours for Studies for the Week		_____

Figure 1. (b) Schedule Card (reverse)

required for each recitation. In column (II) on the back of the card (Figure 1 b) fill in the total number of hours necessary for preparation for each day and for the week.

3. Add items (I) and (II) on the back of the card and find the total hours required for studies for the week. ·It is important to know the total number of hours your studies should require each week according to the curriculum. This will enable you to judge how heavy a load you are carrying. Also, it will aid you in apportioning to other things the proper amount of time. While estimates made by the school for the time required to prepare each subject may not be absolutely accurate, they furnish you with the best possible standard on which to base your plan.

4. Fill in the hours which you are required

to spend on things other than studies and exercise which are absolutely essential. This item
should include time for meals, commuting, outside work, etc. The number of hours which
these things require should be watched very carefully. No matter what school you attend its
minimum will be about 17 hours a week, and its
maximum (for others than commuters) should
not ordinarily be above 22. When it exceeds
this amount it will be worth your while to make
a careful investigation to determine whether or
not that which is requiring this amount of time
actually pays.[3]

5. Fill in the hours which you have decided
to give to exercise, and designate temporarily
those which you desire to give to activities, etc.[4]
Count these up and fill in the total on the back
of the card.

6. Fit the hours of preparation required for
your studies into the hours still left vacant.
Cross out each vertical line in the square as that
particular hour of preparation is cared for. In
case there are not enough hours available to care
for all the preparation, you must, of course, reduce
either item (4) or item (5). *Studies come first.*

---

[3] See Chapter XII.
[4] See Chapters VII and XI.

Making the Most of Your Time

From Monday morning until the following Saturday noon, allowing yourself reasonable time for eating and sleeping, you will be able to find between 65 and 70 hours which you can use. Add items (3), (5), and (6) and see how near you come to obtaining 65 hours. Very few schools of any sort require more than 48 hours of work a week. It would seem a very simple matter for anyone to fit 48 hours into 65. As a matter of fact, the other 17 hours slip away all too easily.

It should be one of your chief purposes in planning your work to compress your 48 hours of study—if this is the amount which you have to do—into 48 actual hours. This will give you more time for play and for other things. To do this you will need to fit each hour of work, as nearly as possible, into the very best hour of time. This is one of the secrets of making a good schedule—a plan which will really work.

Arranging the Hours of Preparation

When you undertake to fit in the hours of preparation you meet with the real problem of arranging your work. By following the previons directions carefully you eliminate as many other uncertainties as possible, and hence make this final step easier. With a little practice it is not dfficult to arrange your study hours to advantage, but it takes time. You cannot hope to accomplish the desired results at once.

First try what appears to be a reasonable arrangement. Begin with classes at the last of the week and work backward, filling in the number of study hours required for each subject you are taking. Work forward, also, when you get stuck. Keep at it until you get all the hours of work fitted in.

Don't be afraid to study Saturday's math. as far ahead as Wednesday night, or Monday's physics on the preceding Friday. This will help you to distribute the week's load and at the same time find which is actually the best time to do the work. Most subjects can be studied to best advantage either just before or just after class. For a few others it is better to put the hours of preparation midway between recitations. Study the prepared work of your classes and determine very carefully the better method in each case.

Incentives

A good way to keep up to your schedule as regards work is to give yourself rewards when you complete the work on time. Keep in mind some pleasant task or recreation which you can enjoy

when the other work is done. In the sample
schedule on page 18 the freshman gave himself
one night off beside his week-ends. This furnished him with additional incentive for putting
through the remainder of the schedule. Also, it
gave him recreation when he needed it. It is a
good policy to follow.

Necessary Changes in the Schedule

All of the writing on the card should at first
be lightly in *pencil*. This enables you to make
the changes which are bound to be necessary. It
is usually best not to ink in even your classes for
a week or so. It is inevitable that shifts in sections shall be made, and these usually necessitate
several revisions of your schedule. Hence it is
well not to be too hasty.

Making Your Plan Work

Try out your plan of work for a week. If it
is absurdly bad, change it after three days, but
you will learn more from sticking to it longer.
Incidentally, your studies will survive the trial
surprisingly well.

After the first week, take an inventory to see
how you stand. You will have learned that your
Chemistry should be studied soon after the lectures, perhaps, and that you can do all your Eng-

lish reading at school Wednesday morning. Make the changes—still in pencil—and try again.

Things will run better this time. However, you will be tempted to cut the corners here and there. You will want to "put things off a bit." Perhaps you are not accustomed to distributing the load over a whole week. If not, you must learn the knack. Don't give up trying. Stick it out and give your studies full time. You will be well repaid in the end.

At the close of the second week fill in your schedule in ink. Do a neat job. You have now planned your work as well as you can. The rest is sticking to it. There will still be interruptions and changes, but these you can patch up. Do not hope for perfection the first term. Make suggestions for improvement on the back of your card, and plan for better results next time.

Other Methods

There are ways and ways of planning your work. I have given you but one. Some fellows feel they do not need a schedule. Others do not want one. A majority of men who do not attempt to plan their work say that they could not follow a plan if they had it. Quite likely they could not. However, the fact that a man does not follow his schedule exactly does not destroy the value of the plan. He at least knows at all times where he stands, and this is the important thing. No one can follow a schedule exactly. It is the man who plans his work and follows his plan in so far as it is possible who gets the most accomplished in the long run.

There is, of course, the other extreme—the man who never plans his work, and in fact is not suited for a technical education at all. An example of this may not be out of place. One man whom I knew never made any pretense of planning his work. About 8 o'clock he would come up to his room to study. For fifteen minutes or half an hour he would dig on mathematics. Soon he would change to physics. Before an hour was up he would have taken a shot at three or four subjects, having knocked off to joke between times. At 9:30 or 10 he would stick on his hat and dash off to the Waldorf for a ham sandwich and a cup of coffee. When he returned, if exams. were near, he might study till 2 or even 3 A. M. Usually he fell asleep, either in bed or on the floor, sometimes studying, but more often reading *Judge*.

Such methods spell failure in your school work. *Get down to business and stick to it for four years.* This is the way to earn your degree.

A Means to an End

On the other hand, the work of your studies is not everything, it is only a part of the bigger, broader education you must get from your four years of training. Your schedule is your plan of work, but you can make it also your plan for play. You must follow it persistently for the most part. You must stick to it nine times out of ten. The tenth time, perhaps, you must break it! In other words, be a man, not an automaton. *You must run the schedule and your work and not let them run you.*

BIBLIOGRAPHY

Adams, John. Making the Most of One's Mind.

Edwards, A. S. Fundamental Principles of Learning and Study. (Warwick and York.)

Emerson, Harrington. Course in Personal Efficiency.

Garth, T. R. How College Students Prepare Their Lessons. (Pedagogical Seminary. Vol. 27, 1920, p. 90-98.)

Gowin, E. B. Developing Executive Ability.

Hazlitt, Henry. Thinking as a Science.

King, I. An Inquiry into Certain Aspects of the Study Habits of University Students. (School & Society. Vol. 2, 1915, p. 824-28.)

Kitson, H. D. How to Use Your Mind.

————Scientific Study of the College Student. (Psychological Review Monographs. Vol. 23, No. 89, 1917.)

Lunt, F. S.   Some Investigations of Study Habits. Journal of Educational Psychology.   Vol. 1, 1910, p. 344-8.)

Mudge, E. J.   Automatisms in Study.   (Pedagogical Seminary.   Vol. 27, 1920, p. 99-100.)

Rowe, S. H.   Study Habit and How to Form It. (Education.   Vol. 30, 1910, p. 670-83.)

Swain, G. F.   How to Study.

Whipple, G. M.   How to Study Effectively.
        (See also under Chapters III and IV.)

CHAPTER III

HOW TO CONCENTRATE

It doesn't make any difference how mean and trifling the thing you're doing may seem at the time, that's the big thing and the only thing for you then.—"LETTERS FROM A SELF-MADE MERCHANT TO HIS SON"

Beginning Right

The extent of your professional training depends largely upon the kind of studying you do. The methods you use and the habits you form in your study are of fundamental importance. This is especially true during your first two years; thereafter you will probably persist in the course you have chosen. If you want to make good eventually, begin right. It may be difficult but it is worth while. There is only one way to avoid vain regrets in regard to studying. See your faults *now,* and correct them.

Physical Preparation for Study

Most fellows are bothered with the problem of how to concentrate. Half of it is a matter of physical and mental preparation for study, and the other half is practice.

By physical preparation I do not mean only

that you must be physically able to work by obtaining proper rest, exercise, and diet. These, it is true, are of primary importance.[1] But your physical surroundings also need attention. First, you must have a good place to work. It is essential to have a comfortable chair (but not too comfortable!), a suitable desk, and the best light possible. These are well worth an added investment of time and money. The man who tries to work in a poor light is almost sure to be handicapping himself more seriously than he realizes. Plenty of fresh air is also essential. Give these details your immediate attention, if you have not already done so. You will be well repaid for the trouble.

Your equipment should be carefully arranged. See that everything you need is near at hand. It is most disconcerting to seat yourself for an hour's work on some engineering problem and five minutes later to jump up to borrow your neighbor's handbook, or to find your own steam tables and your slide rule. Acquire the habit of having at hand the things you will need. It will repay you many times over before you have completed your four years' course.

A condition which often helps one to concentrate is to have the decks "cleared for action" before beginning. Take a couple of minutes at the

---

[1] See Chapter VII.

start to clean up your desk. Next get out your graph paper, drawing instruments, triangles, and textbooks, or whatever you will need. You will then be able to buckle down to your task. By continuous effort you can often accomplish more in forty-five minutes than you otherwise could in an hour.

Mental Preparation

It is even more important, perhaps, to have your brain "cleared for action." Put all cares and worries from your mind. The study hour is not the time to think of errands you must do, or of any engagements you have in mind. Do not let your fancy dwell upon whatever may pop into your head. Concentrate upon the work you have to do. See it in the light of its relation to your course. In almost any job you undertake an ounce of interest is worth a pound of effort.

Working at Maximum Efficiency

You cannot expect to be able to keep your mind centered upon one thing too long at a stretch. Some time ago a man came to me with the complaint that he "could not concentrate." Something was evidently wrong, for his record showed a consistent number of failures. We decided to search out the trouble together. A frank talk revealed at least one thing which was not right and which could be changed. He was trying to put three or four hours of study on a subject in one evening, and he was not one who could concentrate for such long periods. Accordingly we rearranged his work, cut down the maximum time each night to three hours, and planned for him to study no longer than two hours at a stretch on any one thing. The results were remarkable. Within a short time he began to pick up in his work. He found that he could concentrate, and his work improved considerably.

The moral is, you should work hard but not too long. It does not pay in the long run to sit up too late to study. Anyone who becomes engrossed in a problem is tempted to stay up and dig on it until the wee small hours. Use your will power to quit at the proper time.

Interruptions

There is really no defence against the interruptions of a friend who drops into the room when you are trying to study. Here the problem is the same one that you will have in later life. Many of our greatest business men have a marked characteristic in this regard. No matter how fully occupied they may be with their work, they are always ready to see their friends. Yet few really big business men will allow a friend or caller to waste his time with aimless conversation. Roosevelt, it is said, had such a remarkable power in his personality that he would completely dominate an interview. At a certain moment, in the calls which were made upon him at the White House, the visitor would find himself clutching his hat convulsively, and the President, overcoming his disappointment, would manfully bid him goodby! Few of us can ever become such masters of the art of dismissal, but, we can strive to approach this goal.

While there is no real protection against too frequent interruptions by others, much can be done to lessen the annoyance. In the first place, locate yourself where it is unlikely that you will be disturbed. It is not necessary to force your own methods upon others, but you can let it be clearly understood that it is your study hour. When interruptions do come, take them as a matter of course, but do not go out of your way to find them. Make it your definite policy not to disturb the other fellow. If you carry this out consistently, he will not be likely to interrupt you.

How to Study a Subject

An important part of an education comes through observing experience and practice of other men who have done what we .wish to do. Some forms of study are necessarily a matter of memory. When any sort of memory work is encountered it is well to realize that there is a right and a wrong method of memorizing. The wrong method is to memorize by rote. In this one simply connects two things or ideas by incessant repetition. Thus a student might learn the formula for water by repeating the symbols H_2O until he has them firmly fixed in mind. Likewise he might memorize the formula for sulphuric acid by repeating the symbols H_2SO_4, etc., etc.

Tested Methods of Memorizing

The right method of memorizing is by understanding. When this method is used an effort is made to connect new knowledge with what is already known. This should be done in as many different ways as possible. Thus in the case of the composition of water the student would learn that it is made up of oxygen and hydrogen. A laboratory experiment would be used to verify this. By exact measurement the student would establish the volume relationship, and from this there would appear the formula H_2O. The same would be done in the case of H_2SO_4, and so on for other similar cases.

At first sight the second method appears the

harder of the two. Actually, in the long run, it is much easier. In the first method the student must deal with thousands of unrelated facts. By acquiring the habit of relating these facts to knowledge he already has, the student simplifies his task in the long run. Numerous facts group themselves about a few general principles. By mastering these it is made much easier to build up a whole framework of knowledge regarding such a science as chemistry.

In using the logical or understanding method of learning, remember first to associate each new fact encountered with as many familiar facts as possible; second, always try to associate a new fact from the very first with that category of knowledge to which it rightly belongs. It is even harder to unlearn a mistaken relationship than to learn an unrelated fact. Finally, bring to mind as often as possible what has been learned, scattering these reviews over a considerable period of time. The engineer must be able to recall what he knows when he needs the information. This ability can be acquired only through long, hard practice, and now is the time to begin.

Putting Methods into Practice

When starting in to study a subject, make yourself review rapidly the ground you have

covered to date. See how much you can recall
to mind. It is worth your while to spend a few
moments in this way. When you have brought
as much as possible of your knowledge to the
surface, so to speak, you will be ready to begin
work on a more advanced lesson.

At one time or another you will become engrossed in some particular subject which you are
studying. You can then fit other matters into
this and so make them stick. Quite often there
will be some special problem on which you are
engaged. Such, for instance, might be the building of an amateur radio outfit. With this problem in mind you can study with keen interest
considerable portions of your physics and chemistry, to see how they relate to your hobby.
Again, in many of the problems in activities, you
can turn to practical use the methods which you
acquire in your studies. There are few ways
more helpful in impressing upon your mind the
important points of a technical education than to
make practical use of your knowledge as often
as possible.

Developing the Critical Attitude

As time goes on it is important that you develop the critical attitude toward your work. No
matter what you are studying, try to keep your

mind open, ready to question every statement made. It is better to be hypercritical than to accept as fact all that you read or hear. Again and again during your course errors will appear in standard works where they are least expected. I recall a case where a class of more than thirty men worked out a problem given them without one discovering the obvious error it contained. The man who perceives the misprint in the demonstration of a calculus formula possesses a valuable trait. It takes a true critic to find a flaw in that which others have held to be perfect. Such men are rare, and as regards the world's progress, invaluable.

The Seven Devils of Obstruction

To get things done, first get them started. The man who sits at his desk, open book before him, but his head filled with big, dreamy ideas, never accomplishes much. Plan to do things the shortest and quickest way, and reduce your non-productive time to a minimum. The goal of concentration is not a difficult one to attain, once you understand and put into practice the rules of the game.

In your third or fourth year, if not before, read "Developing Executive Ability," by E. B. Gowin. The author of this book analyzes very well the hindrances which beset the business executive. With one or two changes, the "seven devils of obstruction" of the business man apply equally well to the student. They are:

Procrastination.
The big dreamy idea.
Things forgotten.
Interruptions.
Roundabout methods.
Letting things slide.
Just getting by.

BIBLIOGRAPHY

Chorters, Mrs. W. W. Methods of Study. (Mimeographed report on methods used in college.)

Gildemeister, F. Study at Home. (National Education Association. Proceedings, 1909, p. 1009-12.)

Giles, F. M. Sensible Directions for Study. (School Review. Vol. 22, 1914, p. 635-37.)

Hazlitt, Henry. Thinking as a Science.

Hinsdale, B. A. Art of Study.

Kitson, H. D. How to Use Your Mind.

Larson, C. D. Concentration.

McMurry, F. M. How to Study.

Martin, A. S. How to Study. (Education. Vol. 40, 1919, p. 248-50.)

Starch, E. K. Educational Psychology.

VanHise, C. R. Concentration and Control.

(See also under Chapter II.)

CHAPTER IV

HOW TO TAKE NOTES AND USE THEM

The Personal Equation in Note-Taking

There is, in every school, the man who apparently does not need to take notes. I recall the case of a student in a sophomore section in Physics who would sit immovable through hours of explanation of electrcial theory and apparently retain almost all the details without the aid of any notations. Other men prefer to listen attentively to all that is said, and immediately after class compose their notes by recalling and recording the most important points brought out. Such "listening" methods, while possibly excellent training, are on the whole unsafe for the technical student. The memory cannot be relied upon in retaining such masses of detail as one inevitably meets. It cannot be .emphasized too strongly that it is imperative for you to begin the practice of note-taking with the start of your course.

The permanent records which you make of your courses of study are likely to be one of your most valuable sources of knowledge during your undergraduate years and thereafter. No pains should be spared to make them understandable and complete, and to record and file them in such a way that they shall be of permanent value. It is to those who are anxious to meet the requirements of this work in the most satisfactory and least expensive manner that this chapter is directed.

Systems of Note-Taking

Before discussing the actual method of taking notes, it will be well to survey quickly the field of note-taking equipment. An analysis of notebooks and forms, which includes those used extensively by most technical students, is given below:

Type of Equipment	Approximate Size of Page (Inches)
Memindex	2¾ x 4
Lefax	3¾ x 6¾
Fixed-page notebooks...........	2½ x 4 to 7½ x 10
Loose-leaf notebooks.................	2½ x 4 to 8½ x 11
Standard or other size paper with Strapflex binders.................	8½ x 11 or smaller
Standard or other size paper with adjustable clip binder and pasteboard or cloth cover....................	8½ x 11 or smaller

Memindex (pocket memorandum; see also in Chapter V, page 62,) is not suitable for taking notes regularly, but it can be used to advantage to record lesson assignments, and in cases of emergency to jot down the substance of a lecture.

Lefax has a wide variety of forms, **can** be **car**-ried conveniently in the pocket, and its pages are readily filed.

Fixed-page notebooks are seldom applicable in any form to college work except in special cases. The larger loose-leaf notebooks give sufficient space for nearly all kinds of work, but their first cost is likely to be high, and specially punched paper is required for the filler.

Strapflex binders, which are manilla folders with the provision made for binding letter-size paper with common brass fasteners, are conven-ient for carrying separate sets of notes and for filing.

The cheap pasteboard or cloth cover binder, size 9½ x 11½, which, by means of a "clutch-clip" or other simple binding device, will hold all descriptions of paper up to standard letter size (8½ x 11) gives all the advantages of large size paper, elasticity and reasonable cost.

Selecting a Permanent Equipment

In selecting your note-taking equipment for a four-year course it is worth your while to decide upon a form which will meet your requirements consistently from first to last. Many **men find** that, in the long run, the more elaborate **and** more complete systems do not give the all-round satisfactory results obtainable from simpler and cheaper methods.

One very important feature to consider is the size of the page. Any notations or sketches which can be recorded on a small paper can be set forth as well or better on a larger sheet. Neatness, clearness, and completeness are frequently far more desirable in recording technical data than compactness. In all your note-taking a fact worth keeping in mind is the negligible cost of paper, compared with the value of your time.

Making Note-Taking Worth While

The framework for a lecture, or, in fact, for any written or spoken expression of thought, is the outline or list of subjects discussed. In taking notes of a lecture this framework should receive your attention first.

The taking of a simple outline is not ordinarily difficult, but where the complete thoughts of a speaker are to be recorded the problem is different. Some students are prone to take thought notes "parrot fashion"; that is, they receive information through their eyes and ears and simply record it in the same words. This method may be better than none, but the returns to be expected are likely to be small in proportion to the effort expended.

Make your notes similar to those taken by a newspaper reporter and not like those of a stenographer. The man who takes stenographic notes usually files them without rereading or revising, and is not likely to look at them again.

Notes taken properly are a record of your own thoughts and not merely a résumé of what some-one else has said or written. For this reason they are doubly valuable to you. Besides aiding you to digest the knowledge which you wish to make your own, such notes furnish you with a permanent record of your studies.

Notes of Permanent Value

As shown above, an outline of a lecture is likely to be more brief and easier to take than notes including both subjects and predicates. Such outline notes, on the other hand, are of little value unless the actual ideas expressed by the speaker are fresh in the mind of the person reading them. Records that you take in the outline form "grow cold" rapidly. On the other hand, if you will take care to see that valuable data are put in the form of an abstract before filing, it becomes equally valuable to you now or in the future.

The two samples of lecture notes shown below (Figures 2a and b) bring out this point. By reading over the outline in the first case, one gets

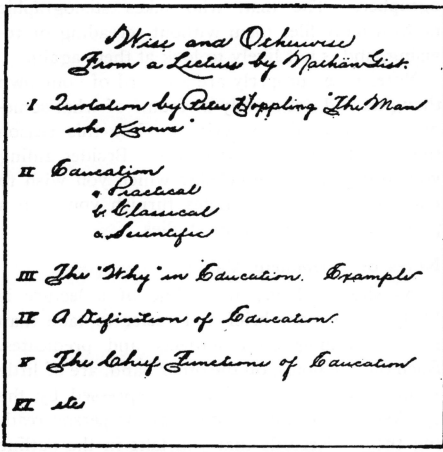

Figure 2. (a) Lecture Notes in Outline Form

a vague idea of what the lecturer had to say. The abstract form, however, has the power to bring to one's mind almost the exact thoughts which were emphasized in the lecture. Your ideal in note-taking should be to put your notes into such form that they can be easily read and understood if reviewed by you five years hence.

Wise and Otherwise
From a Lecture by Nathan Gist

Peter Hoppling says: "Today it is 'the man who knows' whom we need"

Although "Practical Education" is the cry today, Classical and Scientific Education are still fundamentally important

The "why" of things is important
Why do 2 and 2 make 4?

What have you that others have not? Education is finding this out and drawing out your latent talents. Every man is a genius along the particular line that he can do best.

Education should not stuff with facts; it should draw out the ability and talents
Etc.

Figue 2. (b) Lecture Notes in Abstract or Predicate Form

The Use of Shorthand in Note-Taking

Some do not find shorthand too difficult to learn through individual study, but the better method is to take a course in the subject. If possible, avail yourself of this opportunity in high school. Perhaps a summer course will offer an excellent alternative. If the learning of a shorthand system is undertaken at all it is worth while to become proficient. It is then possible to keep in good practice by using this method of saving time in much everyday work.

The danger in using shorthand is that words will be recorded rather than thoughts. By taking the notes in shorthand more time should be made available for thought and attention on what is being said. If notes are taken by this method, and later transcribed in long hand or on the typewriter, excellent results can be obtained.

Systematic Filing of Notes

In addition to taking careful records throughout your course, you should also see that they are properly preserved. Any system of note-filing which you adopt should be simple enough for you to maintain regularly, so that the notes may be readily accessible for immediate reference. Also they should be in such form that all or a part of the material can be moved without difficulty.

Usual Methods of Filing Notes

There are probably as many ways of attempting to file notes as there are methods of taking them. One of the commonest, which many students too often adopt through negligence, is to leave them in a notebook until the end of the term. There is then little time for revision or rearrangement, and in the general clean-up preceding or following exams., the notes are removed from the book and stored in some convenient corner or on an out-of-the-way shelf.

This method of keeping notes is sure in the long run to prove unsatisfactory. The helter-skelter arrangement of the pages makes it almost impossible to find what is wanted when it is needed. Unless a description of the contents is placed upon the package, and the precaution taken to stamp the notes properly with the owner's name, many of the papers are likely to become lost. To get satisfaction from filing your notes, you must be prepared to give the matter serious attention and adhere to a systematic scheme of arrangement consistently throughout your course.

A Practical Method Which Gives Good Results

One can never begin too soon to keep notes in good order. If you desire to do this in a simple, practical way, the following may prove of value:

Obtain first a dozen or so heavy manila folders, size 9 x 11½, provided with tabs which project up half an inch when the folders are upright. Fill in the tabs of as many folders as necessary, using a separate container for each subject. On the outside of the folder can be written or stamped the year, term, and date when the course was taken, together with a list of the textbooks used, etc. This information, while it may appear superfluous, is often of real value later. Above all, be sure that the various sections of the notes are stamped with your name, with suitable instructions for returning when borrowed or lost.

Adaptations to Special Methods

The folders above described are best suited for use with note paper of standard size, 8½ x 11. In case Lefax or any other small-page note system is used, other types of containers can perhaps be used to better advantage. In all cases, however, equal care should be taken to remove used pages from the notebook as often as once a week, and to restock with fresh paper. This removal of pages from the notebook for filing should, of course, be in addition to any regular study or rewriting of the notes. The latter should be carried out, as emphasized above, as soon after the notes are taken as possible.

Storing of Notes

During the term the four or five folders necessary to hold the notes which are being taken
should be kept conveniently at hand. This can
usually be accomplished to best advantage by
standing the folders upright behind the books on
your desk or table, with possibly an extra book-
holder to keep them from sagging. On the other
hand, when the folders are stored, it is usually
best to lay them flat with the tabs protruding so
as to be read most easily. In this way they will
keep their shape, and when reference is made to
any particular set of notes that folder can be withdrawn entirely from the pile.

All of the folders containing the records for a
separate term or year may be bound loosely together. In nine cases out of ten the chronological
order in which the groups of notes are taken
gives the most satisfactory scheme for filing.
With proper care in labeling and storing the folders, excellent results can be obtained in locating
immediately any particular problems or corre-
lated data which are needed for reference.

BIBLIOGRAPHY

Seward, S. S. Note Taking.
Robinson, A. T. Note Taking.

CHAPTER V

SPECIAL TOOLS AND EQUIPMENT

Everybody who ever did anything anywhere had to find the grindstone and run himself against it until he developed an edge that would cut something.—KAUFMAN

Obtaining Necessary Equipment

Throughout your course you will be confronted with the question of what tools and equipment you ought to buy. A student will not always have the exact articles needed thrust before him. In many cases he will not fully realize a need until he has the equipment at hand. He then regrets that such equipment was not purchased long before. In other cases, expensive apparatus will be bought which will be used only a short time and then discarded. In the aggregate the cost of articles so purchased represents a considerable amount of money thrown away. I knew of several men, during my four-year course, each of whom spent from one hundred to two hundred dollars merely on miscellaneous equipment.

In the purchasing of equipment two steps are necessary to avoid making mistakes: first, study your needs, and second, use discretion in purchasing. You must be constantly alert to sense the need for some particular tool which you can use to advantage in saving time, energy, or money. When you have discovered some shortcoming, analyze the trouble carefully to determine how you can best supply the want. Remember that in ninety-nine cases out of one hundred your problem has been solved by innumerable students before you. Employ the principle of "competent counsel" in your selection of equipment. Profit by the experience of others. In this manner you will be most likely to obtain the proper tools and equipment to meet your needs, and you will obtain genuine satisfaction from your purchases.

Investing in a Typewriter

If you have not already purchased and learned to use a typewriter before beginning your course, the sooner you do so the better. The man today who does not know how to use the modern writing machine is handicapping himself, not only in his studies, but also in his work after he leaves school. Plan without delay to make the necessary investment of time and money in order to obtain a typewriter and to learn how to operate it in the most efficient manner. You will be well repaid for your patience and money invested.

The cost of owning and maintaining a modern portable typewriter is not so great as might be supposed. It can be shown that such a machine can be purchased with money borrowed at 6 per cent, be cleaned annually and kept in good repair, and after five or six years be replaced by a new machine, all at an annual cost of approximately $12.50. This is less than 3½ cents a day! A saving of only a very few minutes each day by the efficient use of a typewriter, therefore, would more than repay the student for its cost. The usual rental charge for a typewriter is $20 for eight months. This is $7.50 more than the annual cost of owning a portable machine.[1]

Learning to Use a Typewriter

In order to save time, energy, and patience by the use of a typewriter, it is extremely important that a student should learn the proper method of typewriting. There are two distinct ways of operating a typewriter: the scientific method, called the "touch system," and the unscientific

---

[1] Cost of owning and maintaining a typewriter:

Original cost	$50.00
Redeemable value after 5 years	15.00
Depreciation over 5 years	$35.00
Cleaning and repairs at $2.50 annually	12.50
Interest on original investment, 6%	15.00
Cost over 5 years	$62.50
Annual cost	$12.50

$12.50 / 365 = 3 42/100 cents.

method, sometimes called the "hunt-and-peck system."

While it is often argued by some that a combination of these methods may be developed, there is a clear distinction between the two. In the touch method of writing the striking of the proper keys is accomplished by reflex nerve impulses passing between the brain and the fingers, originating largely from the feeling of the fingers upon the keys. In all other methods of writing the reflex action originates to some extent from the eyes also. The touch method is therefore not only simpler and more rapid, but is much less tiring.

The Touch Method

It is not such a difficult matter to learn the touch method. If you will throw your patience and determination into the task, and attack the problem in the right manner, you can accomplish the desired result without undue effort. It is best when possible to do this during the vacation months, although this is not absolutely necessary. No matter when you purchase your machine, do not count on using it for your regular work, or even for writing letters, until two or three months have passed.

Obtain a book of instructions when you purchase your machine. Follow the directions for learning the touch method. Practice regularly an hour each day if possible. You will learn slowly at first. Use the chart of the key-board, furnished with the instructions, but never look at the keys themselves. Above all, NEVER HURRY. The whole secret of both speed and accuracy in typewriting is taking plenty of time and putting accuracy first.

Mastering the Method

Those who give up mastering the touch system of typing because it is too tedious, may learn to use a typewriter somewhat sooner than the man who persists and wins out. To know the "hunt-and-peck" method is far better than to have no method at all. In the long run, however, the man who learns the most efficient method will far out-distance his rival. He will be well repaid for his greater patience and extra effort. By sliding into the "hunt-and-peck system" a man learns to dash off from 15 to 25 words per minute. But when a man becomes proficient in the use of the touch method, he should be able to write from 30 to 45 words per minute with far less expenditure of effort. An experienced typist, even on a port-able machine, is able to reach as high as 100 words per minute. The touch method is also the more accurate system to use. In order to drive home the importance of accuracy, it may be added that an experienced typist can write fully 25 words in the time which is taken to correct a single error.

Foresight in Learning Typewriting

Men who go through college or complete their technical courses without learning to profit by the use of a typewriter are sooner or later likely to regret their lack of foresight. The amount of writing which it is advisable to typewrite in a four years' technical course is between 50,000 and 100,000 words.[2] In addition there is probably at least twice this amount which can be typewritten to advantage, including personal letters, etc. Work done in this way is of course much neater, more legible, and in general more satisfactory than hand-written work. Usually a student will find that from twenty to thirty reports or themes must be written each term during the third and fourth years. When this becomes true in your case you will be thankful indeed to be able to perform your work quickly and easily on your own machine, instead of having to write it laboriously by hand.

---

[2] Determined by investigation covering all types of courses at the Massachusetts Institute of Technology.

Selecting a Typewriter

Just what typewriter you should purchase is often a puzzling question. A portable model is usually desirable, provided it meets your other requirements. To aid you in selecting the best machine for your purpose an analysis has been made showing some of the considerations to weigh in purchasing a machine:

Qualifications	Weighting	*(Example)	Names of Machines		
Durability	18	10	....	....	....
Standard key-board....	18	15	....	....	....
Performance	18	15	....	....	....
Price	12	10	....	....	....
Convenience and access- ibility of parts......	8	6	....	....	....
Visibility of writing...	8	8	....	....	....
Characters available....	6	5	....	....	....
Weight and dimensions.	6	4	....	....	....
Repairs and other serv- ices by the company..	6	5	....	....	....
Totals..........	100	78			

* The numbers shown here may be varied so as to represent the taste or needs of any prospective purchaser.

Using the Slide Rule

The use of a slide rule is now so common in nearly every technical institution that practically every student adds one of these instruments to his equipment before he completes his first year. This step can scarcely be taken too soon. From the very first the slide rule is likely to prove extremely useful.

There is nothing really difficult about using a slide rule, though practice is necessary to gain speed and accuracy in complicated calculations. The principle upon which the instrument operates is simply the multiplication or division of two or more numbers by the addition or subtraction of their corresponding logarithms. Since the figures on the slide rule measure off logarithmic distances, the addition or subtraction of these distances by placing them side by side accomplishes multipication or division of the numbers. Long series of computations can be quickly and easily worked through on the slide rule, with only a few simple movements of the center scale and slider.

A few suggestions on use of the slide rule are:

1. Obtain a book of instructions and read through the suggestions for handling particular types of problems. Practice the easiest ways of performing the necessary operations for each type, until the correct method becomes a habit.

2. Learn to apply your common sense to the problem in hand, as, for example, in determining the position of the decimal point. Often the easiest way to do this is to point off the answer by a rapid mental calculation, which will also furnish a check upon the reasonableness of the answer.

3. Learn to perform every type of calculation with the least possible number of movements. If the inverted or split scales are on the rule, use should be made of them from the very first.

A Sample Calculation on the Slide Rule

Students will often purchase a slide rule and use it for a year or more without ever learning to profit by many of its labor-saving devices. In fact, there are many very simple operations on even the ordinary slide rule which only need to be described to be appreciated, but which are used by very few students. An example of a problem which is somewhat troublesome if handled in the ordinary way, but which can be accomplished with only four settings and three readings of the rule, is given below.

Divide each of three (or more) numbers, 876, 575, and 143, for example, by their sum, 1,594, and determine what percentage each number is of this sum.

A simple solution of this problem can be effected in this way:

1. Place slider over 1,594 on bottom scale—Scale No. A.

2. Move scale immediately above (Scale No. B) so that 876 is above 1,594. At the left above 1 on A scale, scale read 54.9% on the B scale. *Answer No. 1.*

3. Move B scale to the right till 575 is above 1,594. Above 1 on the left read 36.1%. *Answer No. 2.*

4. Move B scale to the right till 143 is above 1,594. On the right above 1 on the A scale read 8.96%. *Answer No. 3.*

Work the above problem through in order to make sure you have grasped the simple principle involved. The reciprocal method furnishes another way of solving this type of problem, but the procedure given above is usually the more satisfactory.

Selecting a Slide Rule

The polyphase type of slide rule is probably the most satisfactory instrument for general use. In a series of inquiries among men of various engineering courses at the Massachusetts Institute of Technology, 60 per cent of the students used polyphase rules. This is probably true in other similar schools also. Ten per cent of the students used the simplest type of Mannheim rule and approximately the same number used "log log" rules. The remaining students had purchased polyphase duplex rules and others of special types. While many men have special preferences for various types of slide rules, and while certain work can, of course, only be done on special rules, the polyphase will probably meet all ordinary requirements.

A Pocket Memorandum

At times during your course the number of "little things" which you must keep in mind will be large, provided you work at full capacity. You cannot do your best in handling a complex problem if you try to keep all the details in your head. A suitable system of memoranda will aid you greatly here. "Keep the little things on paper and the big ones in your head."

Every man has his own pet system of pocket reminder. If you have not already adopted a system, however, there is one which is fairly standard and which satisfies the needs of the average student very well. This system is called "Memindex."[3] The little black booklet carried in your coat or vest pocket is convenient. Daily cards will remind you of your special errands and appointments for the day. In the other section of the book you can keep separate cards for important personal problems, and for recording ideas. Many students find these convenient also for lesson assignments. A few blank cards give an emergency note-taking equipment which is always ready for use. In many different ways, with judicious use, Memindex or other similar systems of memoranda will help you to "plan your work and work your plan."

A Practical Card File

A second part of Memindex, or of any complete memorandum equipment, is the card file for your desk. This usually consists of a box

[3] Wilson Memindex Co., Rochester, N. Y.

containing one or more alphabetical indexes, in addition to the spare cards for the pocket memo-book.   Such a card file is useful for preserving miscellaneous information and special material which must be kept compactly and referred to from time to time.

Unless one is most careful, an alphabetical arrangement may prove to be a greater hindrance than a help.   At times the indexes nd subindexes in a small desk file may become so confused that it is quite impossible to find what is wanted. Bothering with complicated filing methods is usually a waste of time.

The simple method which I finally used may help you to reach quickly a satisfactory solution of your own particular problem.   This consisted simply in typing ten or a dozen prominent tabs to slip into the main alphabetical index in their proper places.   On each of these tabs was the title of an important section of work or activities, such as "Fraternity" or "Junior Prom Committee."   Whenever the number of cards behind one of the main tabs became inconveniently large, a redivision was made.   To do this the cards were sorted, the worthless ones thrown out, and those remaining divided by means of two or three smaller tabs of a different color.   For example, behind the yellow tab reading "Fraternity" there soon appeared two white tabs which read "House Manager" and "Rushing." The theoretical flaws in such a method are all too obvious. In actual practice, however, I found the scheme required very little time to maintain, and on the whole worked satisfactorily.

Miscellaneous Equipment

In addition to the special tools mentioned above, every student who desires to be efficient in his work should supply himself with other miscellaneous articles of equipment. A number of these are mentioned below. Check over the list to see how many of the articles mentioned you already have, and give thought as to how many of the others you might obtain to advantage.

Pencils and pens
Ink (black, india, red, etc.)
Blotters
Pen-wiper
Ruler
Erasers
Razor blades (for cutting paper)
Clips (several kinds)
Rubber bands
Twine
Letter-opener
Flat desk file (work-organizer)
Letter files

Rubber stamps for name, addresses, etc.
Scissors
Colored pencils
Pencil-sharpener
Library paste and glue
Drawing instruments
Stationery
Scratch-paper
Memo paper
Graph paper, and other special kinds
Paper punch
Book-holders
Desk calendar

BIBLIOGRAPHY

Clark, J. J. Slide Rule.

Collins, C. D. Drafting Room Methods.

Gowin, E. B. Developing Executive Ability.

McClellan, R. Stenographer's Manual. (Niagara Falls, Wahl Printing and Binding Co.) History and Care of Typewriters.

Pickworth, C. N. Slide Rule.

Richardson, G. W. Slide Rule Simplified.

Manuals of Typewriter Companies.

CHAPTER VI

HOW TO PASS EXAMS.

There is only one road to the town of "Success,"
The name of the road is "Work."
                                    —DALE NEWELL CARTER

Common Sense Methods

There is no royal road leading to the passing of examinations. Nevertheless there are certain principles underlying one's preparation, one's mental attitude, and one's physical condition which should be mastered, and when these are rigorously applied the results will often be surprisingly good.

The first principle is to study consistently and thoroughly your subjects throughout the term. This sounds like "old stuff," but it is most sensible advice.

Proper Use of Textbooks

In order to study properly for most courses you must purchase for your own use the books required. It is poor policy to "go halves" with another fellow on books which are worth buying at all. It is even poorer policy to borrow them. Purchase your own books and mark them up all

66

you wish, so as to have them always handy for review or reference.

Proper Use of Notes

The same advice applies to notes. These written records of the course are your own expressions of the knowledge which it holds for you. They are a textbook of which you yourself are the author, and as such you should make good use of them. (See Chapter IV.)

I recall the case of a friend who made remarkably good use of his notes in a certain engineering course. The course was of such a nature that there were no textbooks, and most of the material was presented in the form of lectures. To my friend the subject matter which he was supposed to understand was for the first two months almost a complete mystery. Through sheer desperation, however, he took all the notes possible, although for the most part they were meaningless. Toward the end of the term, however, he began to see some light. By going back over his notes carefully the whole course cleared in his mind. He surprised himself by achieving the mark of "Credit" on the final examination.

Making Up Back Work

During exam. time everyone works under high pressure. A man may be lazy at other times

throughout the year, but not then! Whether the
examinations to be tried are entrance, conditions,
or finals, there is usually too much at stake for
a man to loaf. He is willing to do almost anything at this time that will help him to pass.

If everyone approached the time of examination with work brought up to date, there would
be little need of this chapter. But no one ever
does! At least, the majority of fellows do not,
and these are the ones who need help most.

I recently assisted in lining up an examination
week for a man who estimated that he had an
average of five hours' make-up work for each of
the eight subjects he was taking! In addition
to this he estimated that it would require forty-
five hours to review for his eight examinations.
His case was perhaps not typical, for he was on
the verge of flunking. Nevertheless, many men
find their work in a discouraging state at the time
of examinations.

Preparation by Tutoring

Tutoring gives a student close personal contact
with the instructor. It practically assures a much
more thorough understanding of the work than
can otherwise be obtained. For this reason it is
exceptionally valuable. It should be utilized not
only for the purpose of passing an examination

but also to grasp the underlying principles of a difficult subject. In cases where a student takes care to keep both of these ends in mind, tutoring with a competent instructor should bring excellent results.

When it is a question of flunking or of passing a subject, the additional expense of tutoring should not be considered as an extravagance by either the student or his parents. The amount of such expense for a particular subject rarely exceeds $20. While this may look very large compared to the amount of tuition alone, it is probably less than one-fiftieth of the year's entire investment in the subject.[1] When the importance of understanding the work and of maintaining a clear record is realized, such an addition to the year's investment may well be considered worth while.

Reviewing in Discussion Groups

The possibility of "brushing up" for exams. by combining the resources of several men in a discussion group should always be kept in mind. This is applicable to only certain types of work, but in these it is likely to be more valuable than any other form of review.

---

[1] See Chapter XII, "A Technical Education as a Business Investment."

When arranging for a discussion group, there are two points which it is well to remember. First, make sure that each man brings with him all the material and information that he has collected. Second, have the size of the group suited to the work which is to be done. Three men usually form an effective combination, although the number will vary with different subjects to be studied. If the group is too large, time is likely to be wasted and many will not take part in the discussion at all. When possible a competent leader should be in charge.

Planning an Exam. Week

No matter whether you are behind in your work, or whether you expect to pass your examinations without the slightest difficulty, you will do well to give heed to planning your exam. week. Make the most of the time you have in order to cover your work to the best advantage. There is a science as well as an art to the passing of exams.

Let us suppose that you are confronted at this time with the problem of laying out a more or less troublesome exam. week schedule. Below is a method which has stood the test of actual practice. You will find it applicable not only to examination week but to many other occasions when you must do a certain amount of work within a given time.

A Method Which Works

First, on a sheet of 8½ x 11 paper, make out a list of what you have to do (Figure 3). This should be done, and in fact your whole exam. week planned, several days before exams. actually start. Your list of tasks will look something like this:

WORK TO BE DONE		
	Hours	
	1st Estimate	Revised
Subject A Back Work............	9	6
Subject B Back Work............	4	2
Subject D Preparation for Exam..	4	4
Subject E Preparation for Exam..	8	6
Etc.	etc.	etc.
Totals	81	42½

Figure 3. Program of Work for Examination Week

Notice that you have two columns at the right, one for the first estimate and a second for the revised time. *Fill in only the first estimate now.* Put the hours down in this column which you actually believe you will spend in doing the work reasonably well.

Next, lay out on other similar sheets (or on a

standard schedule card) all the hours which you have available during the examination period. Right here is where the "art" comes in. *Do not fill in too much of your time for study.*

Exercise and Recreation

The sort of work which is required of you during examinations is different from the regular routine. You must make allowance for this. Give yourself at least an extra half-hour of sleep each night. Do not study more than two hours and a half at a stretch. *Get some exercise and recreation every day.* Follow these suggestions to the letter and you will be surprised at the difference in results.

EXAM. WEEK SCHEDULE
TIME AVAILABLE
THURSDAY

		STUDY
7:30	Up (plenty of time for breakfast)	
9-12	Exam. Subject A	
12-2	Lunch and outdoor recreation	
2-3:30	Study	1½
3:30-5	Study	1½
5-8:30	Early dinner and movies	
8:30-10:30	Study	2
11	Bed	

Total for Day.......................... 5

Figure 4. (a) Time Available Sheet for One Day in Examination Week

Figure 4a is a day from an actual Time Available Sheet, made out for a day during exam. week. Study this over carefully and make your own out similarly.

Making Ends Meet

When you have made out a chart showing your plan of work and recreation from the time reviewing begins until examinations are over, you are. ready for the next step. This is to add up your total time available and compare it with the number of hours' work you have to do. Be sure to carry this out as suggested. It will give you an excellent idea of what you are really "up against."

Next begin to pare down the hours of work that you will actually give to each subject. You will find it possible to cut off an hour or so here, and eliminate a task which is not essential there. No matter how seriously you have to cut down the hours of preparation, you must make the "hours available" equal to the "hours of work to be done." You are making the best possible use of your time, and that is all that you can do.

In planning your work make up your mind that you are going to apply yourself as diligently on the review as you do in an exam. There will be few interruptions at this time. An hour's studying, therefore, means an *actual hour of work,* and you should be able to do more in this hour than you usually can in an hour and a half.

Deciding When to Study for Each Exam.

There is one more step, which is sometimes the hardest of all. It may take you an hour or two to shift the periods of study for particular subjects so that the work will be done on time. Never mind how much reviewing you might do in these two hours. It will be worth your while to spend this time and plan your week with care.

By first determining the length of time you are to study on any particular subject, you made it much easier to decide when you should do the studying. Let us say, for example, that your third examination is Physics, on Wednesday. If you have made out no plan of work, it will be difficult to decide just when you may best study for this. By planning your work, however, you determine definitely that you can afford to put eight hours on the review of Physics. Furthermore, you know very nearly the exact hours between Monday and Wednesday which you have available for study. It is not nearly so difficult now to decide just which times are the best. Figure 4b shows a Time Available Sheet which has been completely filled in.

EXAM. WEEK SCHEDULE
TIME AVAILABLE
THURSDAY

		STUDY
7:30	Up (plenty of time for breakfast)	
9-12	Exam. Subject A	
12-2	Lunch and outdoor recreation	
2-2:30	Study. Subject D	1½
3:30-5	Study. Subject E	1½
5-8:30	Early dinner and movies	
8:30-10:30	Study. Subject B	2
11	Bed	

Total for Day.......................... 5

Figure 4. (b) Time Available Sheet Completely Filled In

Various Methods

When actually arranging the times to study particular subjects, many fellows find it helpful to give their most difficult subjects preference. It is usually best, however, not to study any subject too near the time when the examination must be tried. A good rule is either to drop work entirely or to change to some other subject several hours before the test is started. Cramming in a few minor details at the last minute rarely helps you to pass.

There are men in every class and in every school whom no amount of coaching at exam. time can save from flunking—nor should it. But every fellow owes it to himself to fight until the

last and to do his best, no matter how far behind
he may be. It makes no difference whether you
are excellent or poor in your studies, the method
outlined above will help you to win.

Summary

The procedure suggested in this chapter dif-
fers from that of the fellow who tries to study
until 2 A. M. before an examination and never
looks ahead more than two days in his work. It
means putting yourself both physically and mentally in condition for an exam., and this is what
really counts. In a technical course it is essential
that you review your subjects. You can do this
best by hard concentrated effort. But to pass a
difficult exam. you need also to be "in trim" and
"feeling fit." It is the man who, through good
judgment and careful planning, can strike a balance, and achieve both of these aims, who will
win out in the long run. Later he will be able to
open the terrifying envelope and find that he has
passed.

BIBLIOGRAPHY

Blair, F. G. Study and Use of Books. (National Edu-
    cational Association. Proceedings, 1909, p. 852-59.)
Dearborn, G. V. N. How to Learn Easily.
Dillingham, J. D. Study Clinics. (School Review.
    Vol. 29, Jan. 1921, p. 15-16.)

Germane, C. E. Value of the Corrected Summary as Compared with Re-reading the same Article. (Elementary School Journal. Vol. 21, Feb. 1921, p. 461-64.)

————Value of the Controlled Summary as a Method of Study. (School & Society. Vol. 13, .1921, p. 730-32.)

————Value of the Controlled Mental Summary as a Method of Studying. (School & Society. Vol. 12, 1920, p. 591-93.)

Lull, H. C. A University How-to-Study Class. (School & Society. Vol. 4, 1916, p. 961-62.)

Whipple, G. M. How to Study Effectively.

CHAPTER VII

HEALTH AND ENERGY[1]

He who half breathes, half lives.—SANSKRIT WRITER

Maintaining Sound Health

Of all the factors which go for making a success or failure, not only in your college work but in later life, health is probably the most important. While you are spending four years in obtaining your college or technical education, establish firmly the habit of putting your health first.

There are continuous calls for every ambitious man to overburden himself and cut the corners here and there in giving his body its proper amount of care. To neglect these matters in college means to neglect them through life. Sooner or later—and quite likely it will be before you complete your four years' course—you will pay the penalty that may be lasting.

Getting Sufficient Sleep

First of all a student should get the proper amount of sleep. While individuals vary, there are very few men of college age who can do their

---

[1] In preparing this chapter the author is indebted to Dr. George W. Morse and Mr. Frank M. Kanaly for valuable suggestions.

best work on less than seven or eight hours of sleep. There are even fewer men who need more than eight hours.

A refreshing sleep will enable you to grasp a particular subject or the underlying principles of a problem far more easily, for then you can actually tackle your jobs, instead of allowing them to push you. There is nothing more conducive to developing your self-reliance and your initiative, or to advancing you steadily in your work, than to get regularly the amount of sleep which you require.

The best plan is to get eight hours of sleep *each night.* Do not cut the corners, especially during your first two years. While you are a freshman and a sophomore establish the habit of going to bed promptly. The less you deviate from this policy thereafter the better.

Some students have difficulty in sleeping even though they go to bed. After an evening of study some light exercise will greatly relieve mental strain. The use of warm light-weight bed clothing is to be highly recommended. Good health, sufficient outdoor exercise, moderate fatigue, and a will to keep your mind off the problems of yourself and your work after going to bed, are the most effective antidotes for sleeplessness.

The Gospel **of** Relaxation

In addition to obtaining sufficient sleep as a means of keeping your fatigue factor low, follow the "Gospel of Relaxation." Read the excellent little booklet by Dr. William James, "On Vital Reserves," and put his "Gospel" into practice. In discussing several good points in regard to "Yankee Inefficiency," Professor James says:

We say that so many of our fellow-countrymen collapse, and have to be sent abroad to rest their nerves, because they work so hard. I suspect that this is an immense mistake. I suspect that neither the nature nor the amount of our work is accountable for the frequency and severity of our breakdowns, but that their cause lies rather in those absurd feelings of hurry and having no time, in that breathlessness and tension, that anxiety of feature and that solicitude for results, that lack of inner harmony and ease, in short, by which with us the work is so apt to be accompanied, and from which a European who should do the same work would nine times out of ten be free.

Plan your work during the day so that you will have your "daily vacations" as well as your week-end good times. Relax now and then during an evening of study, perhaps by boxing or wrestling, or by taking a run around the block. Break off from your study before you become too tired, and rest for five minutes by chatting with the fellows, before you take up the next job.

When you do desist from your work at all, drop it entirely. The ability to carry heavy loads, but not to worry about them except at the proper time, is one of the most valuable assets.[2]

Importance of Physical Exercise

Next in importance to sleep is physical exercise. From my own experience and observation I believe that in some respects a certain amount of exercise is of even greater importance than plenty of sleep. When your body is full of fatigue poisons you will be surprised at the immediate improvement resulting from a thorough physical workout. The fellow who is not getting a reasonable amount of exercise daily is fatally handicapping himself.

Effects of Lack of Exercise

It is very safe to say that lack of exercise is the cause of far more of both your physical and mental weariness than you imagine. If you feel "sour" at times and disgusted with life in general; if you lack the ambition or the energy to tackle your work from day to day; if you are troubled with a stuffy feeling in your head or a dull ache; or if you are just naturally going

[2] Dr. George L. Walton's Book, "Why Worry?" is one of the best to read on this subject.

"stale" on the job—try getting some exercise and see what a difference it will make. There is no better all-round doctor than Mother Nature, and exercise is her best medicine.

Finding Time for Exercise

The problem which bothers everyone in regard to getting sufficient exercise is how to find the time for it. The answer is, take the time. Put it on your schedule. First, set aside a certain amount of time for exercise in general. Second, apportion this to the various kinds of exercise, in such a way that you will get the maximum benefit and satisfy your individual needs.

In general most kinds of exercise may be grouped in two classes or types. These are home and personal exercises (including walking, morning and evening exercises, etc.) and other forms, such as games, sports, and gymnasium work. Do not confine yourself to one of these types of exercise, but use both to keep your body in proper condition.

What Exercise to Take—Walking

Time spent in walking to and from school is not a loss, provided one makes the most of it. If done correctly, walking is one of the very best forms of exercise. A noted French physician has proclaimed that merely by walking on the balls of the feet (partially on tip-toe) during the course of the day one can correct many physical defects and keep oneself in good condition. Many students who have spent as much as an hour a day for several years walking to and from school, feel sure that they have gained more than they have lost from the added expenditure of time and energy.

Home Exercises

Exercises which can be taken in your room need not consume more than ten or fifteen minutes a day. There are many different methods which are good. If you are fortunate enough to have a phonograph available, probably nothing can be better than the exercise records which may now be purchased. By the courtesy of Mr. Frank Kanaly, who has for several years been Athletic Director at the Massachusetts Institute of Technology, there are given here some simple but thoroughly practical exercises. Make use of these regularly morning and night. They will aid you to keep in first class condition.

FIRST EXERCISE—ABDOMINAL MUSCLES

From a starting position of standing with legs spread about two feet apart and arms extended forward horizontally:

Count 1. Bend trunk forward and swing arms downward between legs. (Do not bend at the knees.)

Count 2. Raise the trunk and swing arms horizontally to the left.

Count 3. Again swing downward between legs.

Count 4. Swing arms horizontally to the right.

Repeating to include 32 counts.

SECOND EXERCISE—INTESTINAL TRACT

From the starting position of lying on the back with hands clasped under the head and legs raised vertically:

Counts 1 and 2. Bend the knees and make continuous foot circles of about 18 inches in diameter.

Repeating to include 16 counts. (While resting after this exercise, massage the abdominal region, using a circular movement of the hands.)

DEEP BREATHING EXERCISE

From a starting position of standing with legs together and arms at sides:

Count 1. Inhale deeply, raising arms upward at sides until overhead.

Count 2. Exhale, lowering arms to side.

Count 3. Inhale deeply, raising arms upward in front of body until overhead.

Count 4. Exhale, lowering arms to side.

Count 5. Arms bent at elbows and extend forward on level with shoulders. Inhale deeply, drawing elbows well back.

Count 6. Exhale. "Pat it out" with the hands.

THIRD EXERCISE—LIVER-SQUEEZER

From starting position of standing with legs and feet close together, and arms extended above the head with fingers clasped:

Count 1. Bend the trunk to the left.

Count 2. Return to erect position.

Count 3. Bend the trunk to the right.

Count 4. Return to standing position.

Repeating to include 16 counts.

FOURTH EXERCISE—TRUNK, ARMS, AND LEGS

From the starting position of lying on the back with hands at the sides:

Count 1. Raise the trunk to vertical position and touch the toes with the hands, arms extended.

Count 2. Return to starting position.

Repeat deep breathing exercise.

FIFTH EXERCISE—LEGS, TRUNK, AND ARMS

From the starting position of standing with legs spread about two feet apart, and arms raised overhead and parallel:

Count 1. Full bend of trunk forward and downward, at the same time swinging the arms between the legs as far back as possible.

Count 2. Return to starting position.

Repeating to include 16 counts.

Repeat deep breathing exercise.

SIXTH EXERCISE—BACK, ARMS, AND LEGS

From the starting position of standing with legs and feet together, and hands at the sides:

Count 1. Full bend knees and place the hands on the floor beside the feet.

Count 2. Extend the legs backward and straighten the arms. (The weight now rests upon hands and toes with face upward and back arched.)

Count 3. Return to same position as Count 1.

Count 4. Return to position.

Repeating to include 16 counts.
Repeat deep breathing exercise.

Bathing and Keeping Clean

After your exercises in the morning especially, take a cold bath or shower. Then rub yourself dry with a harsh towel, making sure that no dampness remains on any part of the body. If a good reaction results from a cold bath it gives an excellent stimulus to the skin and to the whole body, and apparently in many cases aids also in building up resistance to colds and other maladies.

Getting a Thorough Work-Out

For a man to get the most from his body he must frequently have a thorough work-out. It may seem rather difficult at first to knock off for three or four hours a week and give the time to exercise, but try it for several months and you will be surprised at the improvement in your work and in your general health. To some this may savor of prep school days, when gym. was required three times a week. But drop into the gymnasium of your own free will, or join with one or two others in a game of hand ball, and you will be surprised at the enjoyment you get. When such exercise becomes monotonous, and when the season is right, try some lively outdoor sport. Learn to enjoy your work-outs, and take them regularly three times a week. The time so spent will be anything but wasted, and you will be able to perform your other duties better for having taken the extra time off.

Common Sense in Eating

Few men realize the important bearing of proper food and a balanced diet in generating an abundance of physical energy. Danger usually arises from disregarding the counsel of moderation. Students, especially, are likely to eat either too much or too little food. The former may cause trouble, due to the formation of poisons by the partially digested food, and the latter is sure to reduce a student's effectiveness. Eat enough to meet your needs but do not stuff your stomach with more food than you can possibly utilize. In striving to maintain the ideal balance it is well to remember that the amount of food required is practically proportional to the physical exercise taken. It has little to do with the mental activity. Give your body the amount and the kind of fuel it demands to carry on its work. Do not over-supply it with trash which does more harm than good.

It would be absurd for a student burdened with

all his other cares to bother about a balanced diet. Ordinarily the appetite is the best of guides. In the eating of two classes of food, however (proteins and cellulose material), the appetite is of little assistance in determining the proper amounts. In general too much protein and too little cellulose material is eaten. Below are appended some suggestions by authorities on the subject of foods who are familiar also with the needs and failings of the average student:

Eat plenty of fruit, preserved or fresh.

Eat plenty of coarse vegetables.

Eat meat not oftener than once a day. Most students eat twice as much protein as necessary. This includes meat, fish, cheese, nuts, etc. More than enough protein for an average student for one day would be obtained from the following: One egg, one glass of milk, four slices of bread, and six ounces of lean meat or fowl.

Eat coarse bread. Bran muffins are excellent for scraping the intestinal tract.

Drink plenty of water. Eight glasses a day is a good standard.

Eat a moderate amount of pastry and sweets.

Beware of an excess of tea or coffee.

Prevention of Colds

The ravages of colds upon the health and general efficiency of students during a school year are of serious consequence. The tendency among those fighting this menace is toward prevention of the epidemic rather than cure. By giving heed to the details of caring for yourself, you can do much in aiding this work.

An important point to remember in avoiding colds is to keep the teeth and mouth scrupulously clean. Don't spare the tooth brush, either morning or night. A still more serious danger than mouth infection lies in incomplete excretion from the intestinal tract. Gowin speaks of this as the "worst of all anti-efficient maladies." A better treatment for constipation than any amount of cathartic is sufficient exercise, six or eight glasses of cold water a day, and a couple of bran muffins. By keeping your body as free from dirt and poisons as possible, getting plenty of sleep, and by taking precautions against damp feet, either from perspiration or moisture from the outside, you should easily be able to reduce your susceptibility to taking cold to one-third of what it would be ordinarily. This is a long step toward attaining the goal of 100 per cent efficiency in health and energy, which should be every student's aim.

The following suggestions are taken from a paper entitled "Colds and Coughs," by Dr. G. H. Boehmer, of Sandusky, Ohio. After duly emphasizing the fact that colds are not by any means taken seriously enough, either by the average physician or the average patient, the author points out the wide range of secondary disorders, which can be directly traced back to the patient having "caught a cold," and continues:

I think the sooner we quit "kidding ourselves" with the so-called cold cures, the sooner we regard all colds, especially of the respiratory tract, with gravity and anxiety, impress our patients with their complications and secondary disorders and make them understand that isolation and rest in bed is the most satisfactory, quickest and safest cure, we will have gone a long way towards accomplishing something definite, relieving much suffering and materially reducing our death rate.

BIBLIOGRAPHY

Bainbridge, F. A. Physiology of Muscular Exercise.
Camp, W. C. Keeping Fit All The Day.
Fisher, I. Effect of Diet on Endurance.
Walters, F. M. Principles of Health Control.
Williams, J. F. Healthful Living.

CHAPTER VIII

GENERAL STUDIES—READING AND SELF-EXPRESSION

There are two general classes of competency which are generated in the schools. These are Competency to Serve and Competency to Appreciate and Enjoy.—Professor J. B. Johnson. "Two Kinds of Education for Engineers." Waddell and Harrington, Addresses to Engineering Students.

The Importance of Non-Technical Courses

In the curricula of most technical schools at the present time a considerable number of general studies are included. These consist chiefly of courses in English, History, Language, General Science, Economics, and Fine Arts. To those who are unfamiliar with the needs of technical students, the reason for the introduction of such subjects is not always clear. Probably in your case, if you were left to your own resources in beginning a course of technical study, you would eliminate to a large extent all extraneous work and would then feel that you were "getting down to business." In reality, the general studies offered in connection with technical courses of training form what is unquestionably an essential part of the broader training of the engineer today.

The study of subjects other than those dealing with science, mathematics, and the mechanics of engineering gives you a broader basis upon which to build your specialized training. It has been wisely said that the competent engineer should know "something about everything, and everything about something."

Getting the Most from General Studies

There are two ways in which you may regard a general study which you take. Either you may look upon it as a nuisance, and as something to be passed off with as little unnecessary effort as possible; or you may regard it as giving you exceptional opportunities for recreation and broader development. Formerly, such studies may have been irksome to you; now you can go to them for enjoyment and a wider outlook.

Selecting Optional Courses Wisely

The problem of what general or optional courses you should choose is an important one to consider. An acquaintance, who had recently taken work in both a technical institution and a large university to obtain his doctor's degree, emphasized strongly in discussing this subject the necessity for a most careful selection of such courses by technical students, in order to avoid the danger of too narrow technical training. Also, he appreciated the advisability of selecting courses which could not be mastered later.

Self-Expression for the Engineer

In the past it was felt that engineers found little use for anything beyond a cursory training in English composition and rhetoric. At the present and in the future, however, this error is bound to be rectified. The engineer is no longer an isolated calculator of mathematical results, but is called upon to throw himself bodily into the struggle of modern business. For every progressive step that is made, there are contracts to be drawn up, reports to be written, and boards of directors to be convinced. Important transactions, whether of a business or a purely scientific nature, are the results of exchanges of thought. The engineer and the technical expert are repeatedly called upon to interpret as well as to record the findings of their investigations. As one of the broader technically trained men of today, desiring every opportunity for success, you must prepare yourself to meet these requirements.

Means of Improvement

There are many ways in which the technical student can greatly improve his ability to express

himself while he is obtaining his regular course
of training. The reading of good books is an
excellent stepping stone to improvement in the
use of English. The courses customarily given
in English and Public Speaking in most technical
schools are regarded by many students as com-
paratively unimportant. In reality they are of
scarcely less importance than the technical training itself.

Establishing a Goal of Self-Expression

There are two definite goals of achievement in
self-expression toward which you should strive
throughout your course: First, you should be
able to write a first rate report on a technical or
semitechnical subject; second, if given a similar
topic you should be able to address a group of
men forcefully and effectively.

A report is not to be regarded as a mass of information thrown together in writing, nor even
as a fairly well-connected statement of facts and
conclusions. Rather it should be a carefully
planned, logical statement, directed toward the
accomplishment of a definite purpose. Its form
should be standard, the organization and presen-
tation of its material should be effective, and its
English should be clear and concise.

Your ease in speaking should be so well developed through continued training ,and practice that you will be able to address an audience without losing your poise and self-control. Learn to marshal your facts in such a clear, forceful, and unhesitating manner, that they drive home your points convincingly.

Business men who deal with graduates of many of our technical institutions complain that they find them inadequately trained to cope with the human factor. In the future it will be the man who has the ability to express his thoughts readily and convincingly both in writing and speaking who will fill the highest positons.

The Student Engineer and Good Literature

There is nothing better to get your thoughts out of a rut and to refresh your mind and imagination than good reading. Have you ever considered that in reading a book you are usually getting within a few hours the concentrated results of perhaps years of thought and effort by the author? An acquaintance used to say that he could get more real fun out of his Mark Twain than most of us did from the movies. This habit of reading will stand you in good stead throughout your whole life as an infallible means of improving your general knowledge and of giving you recreation and enjoyment.

Finding Time to Read

Students are likely to say that reading is not possible for a man taking a technical course, but I heartily disagree with them. Considerable reading can be done by any college or technical man, no matter how busy he may be. It is largely a matter of filling in the spare moments, and the habit of picking up a good book or magazine and reading it as the opportunity presents itself is well worth your while to cultivate.

There is also the further possibility of making your reading an incentive for completing your other work. Plan to give up certain quiet hours to enjoyable books. Arrange this on your schedule. Soon you will learn to anticipate these and to appreciate them fully. And in the end you will acquire the habit of reading rapidly and intensively when deeply interested.

What to Read

What you read will depend of course somewhat upon the conditions and circumstances of the time at your disposal. The summer offers a good opportunity for the books that are too long to undertake during a school term. I recall an acquaintance who made out a carefully selected list of books to read before he left school after his second year. During the summer he completed the reading of more than a dozen of them.

On the other hand, while school is in session, one book a month is a reasonable standard to maintain. A list of books and periodicals is here added to guide you in a wise choice of reading throughout your four years' course.

Specific Suggestions [1]

The objective of the study of required textbooks is a mental discipline that pushes forward the frontiers of knowledge. The objective of cultural reading is a mental pleasure and a vision that pushes forward the frontiers of life.

SUGGESTED AUTHORS	SUGGESTED BOOKS [2]
Humor	
Mark Twain	Huckleberry Finn
Stephen Leacock	Nonsense Novels
Heywood Broun	Seeing Things at Night
Robert Benchley	Of All Things
Donald Ogden Stewart	Outline of History
	A parody "which makes you laugh aloud when you read it in solitude."
Louis Untermeyer	Heavens
	Parodies by virtue of which "he wins the immortals by his limitations of immorality."

[1] This list of books and periodicals has been compiled especially for "Tackling Tech." by Mr. W. Frederic Berry, Librarian of the *Christian Science Monitor*, Boston, Massachusetts.
[2] In every case other books by the same author are likely to be of equal interest and value.

SUGGESTED AUTHORS	SUGGESTED BOOKS

Fiction

English

Rudyard Kipling	Kim
R. L. Stephenson	Kidnapped
Hugh Walpole	The Dark Forest
	The Secret City
Joseph Conrad	Youth
	Nostromo
Gilbert Chesterton	The Napoleon of Notting Hill
John Galsworthy	The Forsyte Saga
Conan Doyle	Micah Clarke
	The Hound of the Baskervilles
Daniel Corkery	The Hounds of Banba
	An intimate revelation of the soul of the Irish revolution written with rare literary charm.
Alys Eyre Macklin (translator)	Twenty-nine French Tales
	These fascinating *contes* are so many touchstones to the understanding of the French character.

American

Edith Wharton	The Age of Innocence
Willa Cather	O Pioneers!
	My Antonia
Zona Gale	Miss Lulu Bett
O. Henry	The Trimmed Lamp
Don Marquis	Cruise of the Jasper Carter and Other People
Booth Tarkington	Alice Adams

SUGGESTED AUTHORS	SUGGESTED BOOKS
Sinclair Lewis	The Job
Sherwood Anderson	The Triumph of the Egg

Psychology, Philosophy, and Ethics

John Dewey	Human Nature and Conduct
D. Drake	Problems of Conduct
James Harvey Robinson	Mind in the Making
William James	Selected Papers on Philosophy
	The Will to Believe and Other Essays
	Pragmatism
E. B. Holt	The Freudian Wish

Present-Day Questions

F. C. Kelly	Human Nature in Business
W. E. Hocking	Human Nature and Its Remaking
W. L. Chenery	Industry and Human Welfare
Otto Kahn	Our Economic and Other Problems
John Hayes Hammond and Jeremiah Jenks	Great American Issues
Rudolph Eucken	Socialism, an Analysis
Walter Weyl	Tired Radicals
Walter Lippman	Public Opinion
Graham Wallace	Human Nature in Politics
	Our Social Heritage

Essayists
(Best of companions for the odd moments)

Max Beerbohm	More—Works
A. A. Milne	As I May

SUGGESTED AUTHORS	SUGGESTED BOOKS
E. V. Lucas	Adventures and Enthusiasms
John Galsworthy	A Sheaf
Samuel McChord Crothers	Humanly Speaking
	The Gentle Reader
Agnes Repplier	Compromises
Katherine Fullerton Gerould	Modes and Morals
Logan Pearsall Smith	Trivia
C. B. Fairbanks	My Unknown Chum

Nature and Out of Doors

John Burroughs	Camping and Tramping With Roosevelt
	Field and Study
John Muir	The Yosemite
C. G. D. Roberts	Secret Trails
William Beebe	Alone in the Jungle
	Jungle Trails
Theodore Roosevelt	African Game Trails
	Wilderness Hunter
	Through the Brazilian Wilderness

Drama

George Bernard Shaw	Man and Superman
	Cæsar and Cleopatra
Sir James Barrie	The Admirable Crichton
	Echoes of the War
John Galsworthy	Strife
	Justice
	The Silver Box
John Masefield	The Tragedy of Nan
John Drinkwater	Abraham Lincoln
Arthur Pinero	The Second Mrs. Tanqueray
	Mid-Channel

Suggested Authors	Suggested Books
Clyde Fitch	The Truth
	Climbers
Oscar Wilde	An Ideal Husband
	Lady Windermere's Fan
Augustus Thomas	As a Man Thinks
W. B. Yeats	The Hour Glass and Other Plays
Lord Dunsany	Five Plays
William Vaughn Moody	The Great Divide
Charles Rann Kennedy	The Servant in the House

Poetry

Oxford Book of English Verse, ed. by A. Quiller-Couch

Book of Modern British Verse, ed. by W. S. B. Braithwate

Modern American Poetry, Modern British Poetry, ed. by Louis Untermeyer

Chief American Poets, ed. by C. H. Page

High Tide, Songs of Joy and Vision from Present Day Poets, ed. by Mrs. Waldo Richards

Don Marquis	Poems and Portraits
Robert Frost	North of Boston
Rudyard Kipling	Collected Poems
John Masefield	Salt Water Poems and Ballads
Robert Service	Spell of the Yukon

History and Science

H. G. Wells	Outline of History
Hendrik Van Loon	Story of Mankind
Chronicles of America, 50 volumes	Every phase of political, economic, and social development of the United States is treated in this invaluable series.

Suggested Authors	Suggested Books
J. Arthur Thomson	The Outline of Science University of Aberdeen; the aim of this work is to give in plain language an outline of the main scientific ideas of today.

Biography

Edwark Bok	Americanization of Edward Bok
Henry Adams	Education of Henry Adams
Gamaliel Bradford	Union Portraits
	Confederate Portraits
	Portraits of American Women
E. T. Raymond	Uncensored Celebrities (British publicists of today)
Walter Lowry	Washington Close-Ups (American publicists of today)
Lord Charnwood	Life of Abraham Lincoln
A. Rothschild	Lincoln, Master of Men
Bradley Gilman	Roosevelt the Happy Warrior
Hermann Hagedorn	Roosevelt in the Bad Lands

Religion

No books have been added on this subject, not because of a lack of appreciation of its supreme value, but from the conviction that each individual must find the road best suited to his temperament. However, one book—the great book of religion, the Bible—may well be studied. An invaluable introduction to this study is to be found in the "Shorter Bible, Old and New Testament," edited by Pro-

fessor Kent of Yale University. Modern Reader's Bible—
Professor Richard Moulton.

NEWSPAPERS AND PERIODICALS

Daily

New York Times
New York Tribune
New York Evening Post
Philadelphia Public Ledger
Baltimore American
New Orleans Times-Picayune
Chicago Tribune
Chicago Daily News
St. Louis Globe-Democrat
Los Angeles Times
San Francisco Chronicle
Boston Transcript
Boston Herald
Christian Science Monitor

Weekly

The Outlook
The Independent and Weekly Review (constructively a
conservative bi-weekly)
The New Republic (liberal)
The Freeman (high literary standard—advanced radical)
The Literary Digest

Magazines

Scribner's Magazine
Harper's Magazine
The Atlantic Monthly
The Century

Special Features

New York World
Heywood Broun—"It Seems to Me" (brilliant, pene-
trating, provocative)

Franklin P. Adams—"The Conning Tower" (prince of columnists)
New York Evening Post
　Christopher Morley—"The Bowling Green" (stimulating literary persiflage)
The Literary Review (best critical paper in the United States)
New York Tribune
　Don Marquis—Columns
News Interpreters—Worth Reading
　Mark Sullivan
　Frank H. Simonds
　Charles H. Grasty
　Herbert Adams Gibbons
　Crawford Price
　David Lawrence
　Ray Stannard Baker

CHAPTER IX

ACTIVITIES

The Appeal of Activities in College

College activities are in reality very much like high school activities in a more advanced form. They are your old friends dressed up in new clothes. In high school you may never have thought of the Glee Club, school dramatics, the debates, or the athletic teams as "activities." In a sense, all the things of this sort in which you took part, outside of your regular studies and possibly your home duties, could be so named.

Upon your entrance to college or a technical school you find all these functioning, but on a larger scale. The incentive to go out for activities is stronger in college than in a preparatory school, and the benefits which can be derived are far greater. There is a stronger appeal to make good where competition is keen, and the rewards are correspondingly great, but the demands of activities upon your time and energy may be dangerously increased.

Activities for the Freshman and the Senior

The man who comes to a college or a technical school filled with the determination to get the most from his four years of training finds that the term "activities" means more and more as each year passes. The student who has been "through the mill" sees no longer anything mysterious in undergraduate organizations. Although especially familiar with details pertaining to the particular positions which he himself held, he is easily able to picture all the activities of the school and their relationship to one another. In another school, also, he would find little difficulty in quickly grasping the scheme of activities as a whole, and in fitting each group into its place.

The freshman, on the other hand, knows little about activities, except what he learns through the channels open to him. The managership competition or the "chasing of ads." seems of greater importance than the relationship between the Athletic Association and the Board of Student Government. At times he wonders, perhaps, where these detailed duties will lead him. In order to select wisely the opportunities which possibly are open, and to make the most of those so chosen, it is essential that a freshman strive to relate the groups of activities to the whole.

Studying Activities to Advantage

Every man sooner or later realizes that his knowledge concerning activities is incomplete.

There are several methods whereby such knowledge can be improved. The year book at almost every institution is a veritable catalogue describing activities, giving lists of managers, editors, etc., and an excellent idea of the organization carrying various lines of work. Moreover, the names of leaders and others well versed in the various activities can readily be obtained, and these men will converse gladly with younger students eager for information or counsel.

Activities Analyzed

Although the emphasis laid upon specific activities varies in schools, the general plan of student organization is the same. At the Intercollegiate Conference on Undergraduate Government, held recently at the Massachusetts Institute of Technology, striking similarities were evidenced between the main divisions of activities in each of the 42 colleges and technical schools represented. An outline of activities, similar to that used at the Conference, is given below.

1. Undergraduate Government
    Student Councils (Committees, Governing Bodies, etc.)
    Committees and Subcommittees
    Officers (President, Secretaries, Treasurers, Directors, etc.)
    Class Officers

Class Representatives
Class Committees (Junior Prom, Senior Week, etc.)

2. Athletics
Athletic Association (Council, Committees, etc.)
   Officers
   President, Vice-President, Secretary, etc.
   Treasurer and Assistants (or Paid Manager)
   Managers and Assistant Managers
Major Sports
   Football, Baseball, etc.
   Track
   Crew
Minor Sports (Hockey, Gym., Boxing, etc.)
   Cheering Sections, etc.
   Interclass Sports
   Interfraternity Sports

3. Publications
Year Book
Literary and Professional Magazines
Newspapers
Comics
Handbooks
Pictorials
Special Class Papers, etc.
Publicity Relations (reporting to outside papers, etc.)

4. Musical Clubs and Dramatics
Glee Club (regular membership, specialty acts, etc.)
Instrumental Clubs
Bands
Musical Comedies

Dramatics, Mystery Plays
Folk Plays, Pageants, etc.
Management
General Managers and Submanagers
Treasurers and Assistants
Other Officers

Benefits Derived from Training

If you will maintain the proper relation between activities and studies, and between activi·
ties and your other pastimes, the benefits which
you will derive are almost innumerable. You
will be taught to mix with your fellows, to learn
to work harmoniously with many other members
of an organization. Also, you will gain by your
conduct and personality the confidence and respect of your fellows. Thus you will be given
opportunities to develop your initiative, your
"stick-to-itiveness," and your judgment. You
will learn to accept responsibility and authority,
and also to administer them.

You will learn also from bitter experience the
importance of seeking and heeding the advice
both of friends and of enemies. Your interests
will be broadened, and your abilities increased.
In short, if you will but seek to obtain from activities the opportunities they offer, you will gain
from them a large part of the broader education
and training most necessary for your proper development.

The Activities Laboratory

Activities are experimental laboratories, in which, during your four years' course, you can carry out important and valuable study in human engineering. By this means you will learn early to size up yourself by comparing your standards with those of the other fellows. By this process you will learn to test yourself under severe strains, and to receive with equanimity criticisms which are often harsh and biting. In addition you will need at times to curb your ambitions and subordinate your will, in order that through working in harmony with your fellows better co-operation may be obtained. The results of these experiments will give you knowledge of your strong and weak points which later will be invaluable, and which will help you to improve your ability at the time when such improvement is most advantageous. Hence the man taking a technical course does well to go out for activities, and to emphasize in them the spirit of play as much as possible.

Special Advantages from Certain Activities

Certain types of activities give in many cases special advantages to the man who participates in them. This, for example, is true of athletics; for besides the usual advantages to be derived from an extra-curriculum pastime, most of the exercise obtained tends to keep a man in better condition both physically and mentally. Statistics indicate that in technical schools especially, where the burden of work to be done may be particularly severe, a break in the health of students is most likely to occur near the end of the third year. Students who go in for an athletic event for which they must train regularly, inevitably avoid the hazards of not obtaining sufficient exercise.

An Example

Almost innumerable examples of similar advantages might be mentioned. One only will be cited—the opportunities of becoming personally acquainted with members of the faculty and of meeting prominent and successful alumni. In the case of faculty members, more intimate acquaintances are almost invariably established than in the every-day work, and the benefits derived by the student are increased correspondingly.

As an example of such associations the experiences of a friend who recently completed his fourth year at the Massachusetts Institute of Technology are to the point. He filled the important position of Undergraduate Treasurer during his senior year, and he had previously held several others of almost equal importance. While performing these tasks he had come into personal contact with the President of the Boston Chamber of Commerce, the Chairman of the Boston Federal Reserve Board, several other men who were heads of various well-known manufacturing industries, and financial officers of the Institute. Discussions of actual business problems with men of such caliber are bound to be of great present and future value to students.

Résumé

No figures are at present available to show conclusively the effect of activities upon men in engineering professions. Nevertheless, statistics indicate that as many as two-thirds of the eminent engineers in the country took at least some part in functions of this sort during their four years of training.[1]

Many educators are awakening to the importance of the really valuable training which men receive in activities. A report covering an exhaustive research into this matter at the Massachusetts Institute of Technology surveys the field

---

[1] A report compiled by Professor Raymond Walters, Dean of Swarthmore College, through the American Association of Collegiate Registrars, states that out of approximately 180 eminent engineers whose undergraduate records were studied, 61 had taken some part in athletics, 122 in literary and scientific activities, and 115 in social organizations.

from various angles. On the question of how activities are regarded by prospective employers of engineering students, opinions from the heads of courses were obtained. Fairly stated, the consensus of these opinions was that a man prominent in activities and of reasonably high scholastic standing was in greater demand by outside business organizations than one showing extraordinary ability only in his professional work.

The time may yet come when credits will be granted for satisfactory work performed in activities, as well as that done in the more regular courses of training provided by our educational institutions. Both at the Carnegie Institute of Technology and at the Massachusetts Institute of Technology the feasibility of granting a certain amount of scholastic credit to activities by means of a point system is being seriously considered.

CHAPTER X

PLAYING THE ACTIVITIES GAME

Getting a Good Start

College training is valuable because it encourages and indeed forces men to undertake a wide variety of duties, and minimizes the cost of damage wrought through mistakes. Similarly, activities encourage a man to shoulder heavy responsibilities and to perform difficult tasks, and at the same time heap most of the rewards for success and penalties for failure on the individual. You may go out for an activity, therefore, secure in the knowledge that if you do not succeed in your effort few others will suffer as a result of your failure.

It is not essential that a man have great inherent ability in order to go out for a particular activity. Activities afford opportunities for a man to try himself out and to develop ability along various lines. You may soon learn that you are entirely unsuited to that which you first attempt, but this knowledge itself is valuable. By careful selection and by sticking to the search you will find eventually something which you like, and something in which you will be able to make good.

Having an End in View

While it is well to have some definite goal in activities, this is by no means essential. Many men, simply by following the courses open to them, have made remarkable records. Nevertheless, it is wiser to have some specific end in view—some office, not too far beyond your present capacity, which appeals to your ambitions and results in experience enabling you to seize advancement when it comes.

Tackling Detail Duties

No matter what branch of activities one enters, there will be at the start considerable hard work to be done. The seemingly insignificant duties must be handled and performed satisfactorily, if you are to have a chance later at the worth-while positions. Many times these preliminary tasks are objectionable, so that you feel dissatisfied with the work in hand. Nevertheless, keep your eyes on the goal ahead. If it is worth the effort, stick out the grind of the competition and fight unceasingly to win.

The case of a friend who detested above all else "ad.-chasing" for a competition in which he was entered is to the point. Time and again this man would visit the business section of the city, with the intention of obtaining ads., and, because of his loathing for the task, would return without having made a single call. Finally, he schooled himself to do the work, and as the competition neared its end he began to make more rapid progress. During the final week he collected more advertisements than the fourth highest man had obtained throughout the whole time. In the end he actually broke all records for the number of ads. collected, and after serving a year as treasurer of the publication he was finally elected to the position of editor-in-chief.

Studying the Other Fellow

From first to last many of the most important lessons you can learn will come from studying your fellows. This habit is valuable in any branch of your work or play, but especially in activities. Here you are given countless opportunities to study human nature, and by all means you will want to make the most of them. Sooner or later you will be given positions of authority which involve the control and direction of men. It will be imperative that you handle these men ably, and this requires first that you understand them. Moreover, within a short time it is inevitable that your opinion should carry weight in selecting men to fill your own or other positions.

Proficiency in judging and selecting men is of

great importance, as was especially necessary in the case of one position in activities which I have in mind. Here one man was responsible for the selection of half a dozen committees and chairmen of committees, besides having to appoint numerous other men to special positions. The larger the circle of friends with which you surround yourself and the clearer your perception of ther characterstics, the more you will gain from activities and the more valuable service you will render.

Getting the Habit of Success

There is a trite old saying which is even truer here than in most other branches of college work, that "nothing succeeds like success." The attitude to assume in attacking your problems is to determine to make good in your every undertaking. You will thus continually gain ability to handle successfully larger and larger responsibilities.

One of the most successful men I have known in college activities was exceptionally quiet and unassuming in his manner, but had the remarkable gift of getting things done with extraordinary ease. This man was most particular not to call any job complete until its every detail had been worked out. He played the game of activi-

ties skilfully and fairly, and with the strictest ob-
servance of the rules.   As a result he was able to
hold a commanding position among his fellows.

CHAPTER XI

HOW MUCH TIME TO DEVOTE TO ACTIVITIES

Giving Activities Their Proper Place

There are at least two arguments favorable to activities which make them well worth while. Every student whose nature responds to their competitive and social appeal will derive sufficient pleasure and recreation from activities to repay him for the time and energy he expends on them. In addition there is the valuable training received, and the development of interests outside the sphere of study. These alone, as has been pointed out in the preceding chapters, make some participatiou in activities of almost immeasurable worth, especially to the technical student.

Nevertheless, while it is important that activities be given their proper place, studies should come first. If in your own case, for example, you are attending a technical school, your primary motive is not to gain experience in activities, no matter how valuable you may consider this experience to be. The first reason for coming to such a school is to gain a thorough knowledge regarding the principles and practice of Mechanical Engineering, Electrical Engineering, or some similar profession. This cannot be done if the time spent on activities is allowed to interfere too seriously with studies.

Every man who goes out for activities assures himself that he knows the secret of keeping them in their place. Nevertheless, there are few men that are not open to criticism on this score. The excellent "point systems" which have been adopted in so many schools cannot be too closely observed nor too strictly enforced. Besides this check, each man must study his own case carefully. To maintain a proper balance between studies and activities is a problem which is worthy of your most careful consideration throughout your course.

Going Out the First Year

Many men, upon entering a technical school where the courses are likely to be rigorous, hesitate to go out for activities during their first year. There are, of course, the difficulties of getting settled and becoming accustomed to the new environment, as well as the uncertainty as to the amount of time required by studies. These factors naturally cause a freshman to hesitate before plunging into activities at the start. While in some cases good reasons may exist for adopting the policy of waiting, there are several arguments which favor trying out for activities in the first year, and these should not be overlooked.

While for the most part a student can take up any activity at the beginning of his second year and have a chance to make good during the three years that follow, there are a few activities which require consistent work during all four years. Such, for example, is the "Tech. Show" at the Massachusetts Institute of Technology. When this is the case it is imperative from the point of view of activities that a student should begin work in them in his first year. Nearly every activity offers the best opportunities to the man who enters the game early in his course, for in this way an additional amount of experience is gained.

On the whole, any man who has been active in school affairs outside of his studies in preparatory schools can continue naturally to follow the same course without undue effort immediately upon coming to college; while a student who has neglected activities previously finds himself more and more fearful of taking the initial steps as each year goes by. Hence in either case, from the point of view of activities alone, greater benefits can be derived by entering activities the first year.

Waiting Until the Second Year

As stated previously, there are also arguments advanced for spending little or no time on activities during the first year. Theoretically, keeping out of activities for the first term or two should enable a man to make a more advantageous start in his studies. Except in special cases, however, it is doubtful whether better results can be obtained in this way than through a moderate participation in activities. Statistics secured at the Massachusetts Institute of Technology indicate that the standing of all students taking part in activities is actually higher on the average than of those not taking part. It seems plausible to suppose that the recreational effect of activities tends generally to stimulate the interests and efforts of students in studies, as well as in other work.

It is unquestionably true that by waiting until the second year before entering into activities a student is enabled to survey the field more carefully, and later to select work which will best suit his particular inclinations and abilities. At the same time the best way to learn about activities is actually to take some part in them.

The Danger of Overloading

You must decide for yourself when and to what extent you desire to take part in activities. In general, it is a wiser policy to begin moderately with activities during your freshman year, than to attempt to crowd too many outside interests into the remaining three years of your training. The work of activities is in many cases so fascinating that once a man enters fully into the spirit of the game he is likely to be swept completely off his feet. There are two situations in which you will repeatedly find yourself with respect to activities. Either you will be working hard to take some larger part in the game, or you will be struggling to avoid added responsibilities and to meet the obligations you have already undertaken. The latter condition is the more serious, since, unless you are successful in avoiding the severe burdens that may be thrust upon you, your studies are likely to be slighted.

Temptations Met

The dangers which you will incur from overloading with both activities and studies occur in a number of ways. At times when you are carrying more than enough work in activities, an opportunity will appear for you to take up some especially interesting and valuable work. Or, if you are in the earlier stages of the game, you will be asked to perform some special duty which will open unusual opportunities for you in the future. It is difficult to refuse such offers, when a refusal invariably means that the opportunity is lost forever. Nevertheless, at more opportune times other openings will appear. The man who shows himself worthy of advancement when he is ready to receive it must also be willing to refuse responsibility when he is unable to shoulder it.

Another danger is that of finding that unforeseen requirements, either in studies or activities, prevent the completion of important tasks which must be performed before a given time. Such, for example, are the clean-up duties in activities which almost invariably come a week or two before exams. Limit the time which you put on activities near examination times and at other critical periods even more carefully than you ordinarily would. If necessary, cut the activities for a time, and give your entire attention to studies.

Here, as in later life, it is the man who can put aside play when it is time for work, and can forget his work when it is time to play, who will succeed in the long run.

Avoiding an Overload [1]

There is a way of avoiding overloads, which if used more extensively would benefit the cause

---

[1] See Chapter II.

of activities as a whole. This is to turn over to other men not in activities some of the authority and responsibility which you are able to acquire. This will result not only in reducing your load and in giving you the experience of getting others to work, but will also increase the number of men who take part in activities.

One way to avoid putting too much time on activities is to measure the time spent. Usually there are between fifteen and twenty hours a week available for work other than studies. From one-third to one-half of this can wisely be spent on activities. The overburdened schedule of activities defeats its own purpose. The man who is so busy with detail duties that he cannot take time to think or to exchange ideas with his fellows, neither gives nor obtains the maximum benefits. Maintain control of your machine, no matter how interesting or exciting the race may be. Often it is necessary to apply the brakes, and sometimes even to stop. It is the man who drives steadily and hard, in activities as well as in studies, who is bound to come in strong at the finish.

CHAPTER XII

A TECHNICAL EDUCATION AS A BUSINESS INVESTMENT[1]

Difficulties and Advantages of the Comparison

It is difficult for some to think of a college or a technical education as a business investment. The sacrifices which must be made are usually measured merely in terms of money spent. This is because several years must pass after the first investments are made before financial returns are realized. Many of the returns are intangible and uncertain in quantity, so that they can be neither measured nor predicted with accuracy. For these reasons it is not easy to regard a technical education as an investment, and to look forward definitely to the tangible returns it will yield.

Technical Education versus Four Years' "Experience"

If one is to consider an education as an investment, other factors must be taken into account besides money expense.

---

[1] It should be noted that it is not the purpose in this or in other chapters of this book to contrast the technical course of training with that of a liberal arts education. While the figures used are necessarily based upon graduates from a technical institution, much of the information here given is equally applicable to men in all universities and colleges.

The amount of time and energy which a student invests, and the amount of experience which he sacrifices, must also be considered. To show this it is necessary to compare the case of the man who attends an engineering school for four years with that of the man who begins his business career immediately after leaving high school. When this is done the investment of the former is seen to be even larger than might at first be supposed.

Necessary Assumptions

In order to make the comparison possible it is first necessary to make certain assumptions in regard to income and expense. While the figures used here are arbitrary, they have been carefully considered and checked from several angles, and in all probability approximate closely the figures for the average individual. The assumptions made are as follows:

1. The earning power of an average high school or preparatory school graduate upon leaving school is placed at approximately $800 annually ($15 a week). During the next four years it will be assumed that he can earn altogether $3,800 (an average of $18.25 a week).

2. The living expenses of the high school graduate over the period of four years will be placed at approximately $3,200 (an average of $15.40 a week).

3. The expense of a school year at a technical institution will be considered as approximately $1,200.[2]

4. A technical student's net savings for summer work during his four additional school years may be placed at $400.

Tables of Comparison

On the basis of the preceding assumptions, the following tables may be drawn up and then compared:

SALARIED POSITION FOR HIGH SCHOOL GRADUATE
Earning power at nineteen, $800

	INCOME	EXPENSE
1st year salary and expense........	$ 800	$ 800
2nd " " " "	900	800
3rd " " " "	1,000	800
4th " " " "	1,100	800
Total income and total expense...	$3,800	$3,200

Difference between income and expense, $600

---

[2] At the Massachusetts Institute of Technology the minimum for men under ordinary circumstances (not living at home, etc.) is between $900 and $1,000 (1922-23). The amount for living expense ranges all the way from these figures to $1,500 or more. An analysis of these figures can be made as follows:

Tuition	$150-	$300
Clothing, laundry, etc.	125-	200
Room rent	100-	175
Meals	250-	350
Recreation, Week-ends, etc.	75-	150
Books, Fees, etc.	100-	125
Travel and miscellaneous	100-	200
Total	$900-$1,500	

The amount of tuition will of course vary for different schools. See table in Chapter I, pages 12 and 13.

TECHNICAL EDUCATION

	INCOME	EXPENSE
1st year total expense...............	....	$1,200
2nd " " "	....	1,200
3rd " " "	....	1,200
4th " " "	....	1,200
Interest expense at 6%*............	....	720
Net savings from summer work.....	$400	....
Total income and total expense..	$400	$5,520

Difference between income and expense, $5,120

Difference in cost between work for a salary and obtaining a technical education, $5,720 ($5,120 + $600).

* Calculated as follows:

$$\begin{aligned} \$1{,}200 \times 4 \times 6\% &= \$288 \\ 1{,}200 \times 3 \times 6 &= 216 \\ 1{,}200 \times 2 \times 6 &= 144 \\ 1{,}200 \times 1 \times 6 &= 72 \\ \hline &\$720 \end{aligned}$$

Computing the Difference in Cost

In this way it is a simple matter to determine the difference in cost between a technical education and four years of work at a salary. From the above figures it is evident that the man who chooses to obtain four years' experience rather than a technical course increases his assets by $600. The man who spends the four years gaining a technical education decreases his assets by $5,120. The total difference is therefore $5,720, which is in this case the amount of additional cost to the man who chooses an engineering education.

Calculating the Money Value of a Technical Education

In addition to finding the cost of a technical education, it is interesting to compute what such a training may be worth to an average student. It will be seen from the table opposite that the present value of the income of the average technical graduate is approximately $38,700. The significance of the term "present value" is as follows: If the sum of $1,390, for example, should be set aside for a student at the time of his graduation, and if the interest upon this were compounded annually at 6 per cent, the amount of money available from this fund after twenty-five years would be $6,000. This is the amount estimated to be his salary for that year. Hence the "present value" of a $6,000 income which should be received twenty-five years hence is $1,390. As shown by the table, the sum of all the present values for the twenty-five-year period gives the total present value of the income to be received. [3]

In the same table the present value of the salary of a high school graduate four years out of school is also shown. The difference between the mean values of the two series of income is $13,371. That is, during the four years that the

---

[3] The method and figures used in the table are conservative. In some cases the income received would be several times as great as shown.

PRESENT VALUE OF INCOME OVER A PERIOD OF TWENTY-FIVE YEARS.

High School Graduate		Years Out of School	Age		Technical Graduate*	
Range of Income	Present Values†				Range of Income	Present Values†
$1,200–$1,300	$1,130–$1,220	5	22	1	$1,200–$1,500	$1,130–$1,410
1,300– 1,400	1,150– 1,240	6	23	2	1,500– 1,800	1,300– 1,600
1,400– 1,600	1,170– 1,340	7	24	3	1,800– 2,100	1,510– 1,760
1,500– 1,700	1,190– 1,340	8	25	4	2,100– 2,400	1,660– 1,900
1,600– 1,800	1,190– 1,340	9	26	5	2,200– 2,600	1,640– 1,940
1,700– 1,900	1,190– 1,330	10	27	6	2,400—2,800	1,690– 1,970
1,800– 2,000	1,190– 1,330	11	28	7	2,600– 3,000	1,730– 1,990
1,900– 2,100	1,190– 1,310	12	29	8	2,800– 3,200	1,750– 2,040
2,000– 2,200	1,180– 1,300	13	30	9	3,000– 3,400	1,780– 2,130
2,000– 2,300	1,160– 1,300	14	31	10	3,200– 3,600	1,790– 2,140
2,000– 2,400	1,050– 1,270	15	32	11	3,500– 4,000	1,840– 2,110
2,000– 2,500	994– 1,260	16	33	12	3,500– 4,200	1,740– 1,990
" – "	939– 1,170	17	34	13	" – "	1,640– 1,880
" – "	885– 1,110	18	35	14	" – "	1,550– 1,770
" – "	834– 1,040	19	36	15	" – "	1,460– 1,670
2,000– 3,000	788– 1,180	20	37	16	" – "	1,380– 1,580
" – "	743– 1,110	21	38	17	" – "	1,300– 1,470
" – "	701– 1,050	22	39	18	" – "	1,230– 1,400
" – "	661– 994	23	40	19	" – "	1,160– 1,320
" – "	623– 936	24	41	20	3,500– 5,200	1,090– 1,620
" – "	588– 882	25	42	21	" – "	1,030– 1,530
" – "	556– 831	26	43	22	" – "	972– 1,450
" – "	523– 786	27	44	23	" – "	915– 1,360
" – "	494– 741	28	45	24	" – "	864– 1,290
" – "	465– 700	29	46	25	3,500– 6,000	815– 1,390
Totals	$22,584–$28,210	$38,768			**Totals**	$34,987–$42,580
		25,397				
Mean	$25,397	$13,371			**Mean**	$38,768
		Difference				

*Although figures for college graduates are not available, the above could probably apply with only slight changes.

†These values are calculated on 6% basis, compounded annually, accurate to three places.

technical student has spent in gaining his further training he has added over $13,000 to the value of the income he may expect to receive. This amount we shall now consider to be the actual additional value to the student of the investment he has made.

What It Costs to Loaf

An interesting computation can now be made of the cost and value of the available working hours of the day. In other words, we can now determine what it costs an average student to loaf!

In Chapter II it was shown that any student will have difficulty in finding more than 65 hours of available time for work each week. Assuming that there are thirty weeks in the school year, we find that the actual cost of each available hour is something over 70 cents. ($5,720/65 $\times$ 30 $\times$ 4 = \$.73.)

The *value* of a working hour can also be computed, based upon the present value of the additional income during the first twenty-five years after graduation. The figure for this is approximately $1.70. ($13,371/65 $\times$ 30 $\times$ 4 = \$1.71.)

These figures should be kept in mind by students when considering the advisability of obtaining outside work while in college. The remuneration received for such work is frequently less than 50 cents an hour. There are, of course, some cases where earning a little money in this way may be advisable or a matter of necessity. Nevertheless, it is well to remember that the spending of a large amount of time in this way is almost sure to be a poor business policy. As shown above, the cost of the time for an average student is one and a half times the probable earnings, while its value under the same conditions is more than double the cost.

What It Costs to Cut Classes

Incidentally the following points are worthy of note. If the entire burden of expense during the school year be charged to class hours it is found that the *cost* of *one class hour* is over $2.[4] The assumption that classes should be charged with the entire expense might be questioned, since much valuable training may be derived in other ways from the school connection. Nevertheless, the gaining of a technical training is the primary motive for attending a technical school, and it is for this that the student pays. And the *value* of a class hour, based upon the future income, is even greater; it is approximately $4.75. ($13,371/700

[4] This is based upon an average of 700 class hours, as at the Massachusetts Institute of Technology. ($5,720/700 x 4 = $2.04.)

× 4 = $4.77.) With the cost and the value in dollars alone of each class hour so high, students would do well to consider carefully the advisability of cutting classes.

Does the Investment Pay?

In summing up the calculations made for the cost and value in dollars of a typical technical education, interesting conclusions develop. The cost of the four years of additional training, compared with the four years spent by the high school graduate working, was seen to be $5,720. At the time of graduation for the technically trained man, the value of his income for the next twenty-five years had been increased by $13,300. A gain of approximately $7,500 in the present value of the income over and above all additional expense had been made, therefore, by taking the technical course. ($13,300 — $5,720 = $7,580.)

It is not the purpose of this chapter to overemphasize the money value of either a college or a technical education at the expense of the many other benefits which are to be derived from such courses of training. At a recent dinner of a class of technical graduates at their thirty-fifth reunion, nearly half of the fifty-six members of the class were present. It is at such times that the broader value to men of four years of intensive training and of their association together is brought to light. It could not be said that it was the amount of the salaries received which brought the greatest feeling of satisfaction. As each man was called up to rise and give in his own words a brief history of his experiences since graduation, the deepest gratification came from the thought that each and every one had been of some signal service, not only to those who had given him his education, but also to his country. It is the promise of such accomplishment, coupled with the incentive of assured financial returns, which in the last analysis prove that either a technical or college education is a sound investment.

CHAPTER XIII

FINANCING AN EDUCATION

Making the Two Ends Meet

In every engineering school or college there are men who need to have no concern over financial matters during the time they are in school and other men to whom the problem of financing an education is of primary importance. Those in the second group must give careful consideration to the various ways and means of making ends meet, for only by careful thought can they select the methods that meet their special needs.

The problem of financing an education divides itself primarily into two parts: first, the question of obtaining money; second, that of cutting down expenses. This chapter considers the problem of securing the necessary funds.

Importance of Good Marks—Scholarships

The man who undertakes to go through college or a technical institution under difficult financial conditions often does not realize until too late the importance of maintaining a clear record in his studies. In this regard he will be wise to aim as high as possible, and to try definitely for a scholarship. There is a closer relation than is usually realized between maintaining good marks in studies and reducing the cost of an education to a minimum.

In the first place, scholarships offer an excellent source of income, for aside from the extra studying necessary to obtain good marks no additional time is consumed in trying for a scholarship. This is really an important consideration, since, as has been pointed out, a man's time in college is very valuable. Any extra time spent in studying is certainly not to be considered wasted.

The amount provided by scholarships varies widely with different schools, and with the conditions surrounding each case. Scholarships are, however, usually large enough to make quite a reduction in the yearly expense. At the Massachusetts Institute of Technology, out of 331 men who applied for scholarships in 1921 more than half received a grant,[1] and the average amount of a scholarship was approximately $155.

The Additional Cost of Making Up Failures

For the man who finds it difficult to make ends meet, there is another reason why he should

---

[1] Both the marks and the needs of each applicant are carefully considered in the granting of all scholarships at the Massachusetts Institute of Technology.

"play safe" in regard to his studies. This is the fact that if he fails in his work he must either attend summer school or return for a fifth year. These are doubly expensive propositions, for in either case a man should be earning and saving money instead of paying money out. The calculation below shows, by comparing the expense of summer school for six weeks with working the same length of time, that the former may easily represent an added investment of $250.

SUMMER SCHOOL
Expenses:
Tuition (estimated)................... $ 65.00
Living and miscellaneous............. 135.00

Total $200.00
Income 0
Net expense....., ... $200.00

SUMMER WORK
Expenses:
Living and miscellaneous............. $100.00
Income:
Earnings 150.00

Net savings........................ $ 50.00
Difference in cost.................. $250.00

Borrowing Money for an Education

There are many serious misconceptions among college students in regard to the question of borrowing money for financing a higher education. These misconceptions often lead men to handicap themselves in obtaining what they should from a college or technical training. When Shakespeare put into the mouth of Polonius the admonition, "Neither a borrower nor a lender be," he never intended that it should apply to the student who borrows for the sake of investment. True, care must be taken that through borrowing one does not "dull the edge of husbandry." It is perhaps easier to go too far in borrowing, once the way is opened, than not to borrow at all. On the whole the problem of the student who must finance his own education is not to decide whether or not he should borrow, but to determine where, when, and how much he can borrow, without too heavily discounting his future.

Ways of Borrowing While in College

The three most hopeful sources of income for men who wish to borrow money for a college education are: friends and relatives, school funds, and business men who may be interested to lend assistance in particular cases. Without any actual proof of ability to make good in a technical school or college it is often difficult for a prospective student to obtain a loan. Much may often be accomplished among his closer friends and relatives, however, since they are the ones best informed as to his ability and character. A small loan at the beginning can generally be used as an opening wedge for obtaining further assistance when needed. The one-year program is one of the best bases upon which to approach a business man for a loan. It is considered more in detail at the end of the chapter.

It is often quite possible for a student to approach a business man who has the facilities for obtaining money and to persuade him to lend needed assistance. Usually such a man understands the risks involved and will want some reasonable assurance of the success of such a venture. This can often be obtained from a study of past records, or from a showing made in six months or a year's work outside of school.

Reducing the Risk

After a student has been successful in obtaining a loan for educational purposes, both he and the one from whom the loan is secured will do well to reduce all possible risks to a minimum. One way of accomplishing this is to take out a life insurance policy for the student, payable to the creditor, making the face of the policy at least equal to the amount of money borrowed. By deducting the amount of the premiums from the loan when it is made, the premiums may be paid in advance. The best means of reducing the possibility of failure by the student, as well as the risk of loss by the creditor, is to free the student from all handicaps, such as the necessity for earning money or for cutting down too closely on living expenses, during the first school year.

Borrowing Too Little

While visiting a university in New York State recently I came across an old high school acquaintance who was working his way through college. He was then just finishing his sophomore year. During his freshman year, if the scholarship he had been granted were taken into account, he had actually earned enough money to pay all expenses and to go home with $25 in his pocket. His miscellaneous expenditures, he told me, averaged less than $1 a month! In his second year he was granted a larger scholarship and with this added assistance he was able to save the sum of $50 between December and April. The time he had spent on outside work each week was over twenty hours. His remuneration had amounted to $2 a week plus room and board, or approximately $12.[2]

---

[2] This figure might be considered rather high for some institutions. Between $9 and $11 can be earned on similar work at the Massachusetts Institute of Technology.

This fellow, who was of German descent, undoubtedly carried industry and frugality to the extreme. The point I wish to make is that he did so under the firm conviction that his method was the very best possible. In fact, it was the only way, as he saw it, for him to gain a college education without putting himself under objectionable obligation to anyone. At the end of his first year he had been given several opportunities to borrow as much money as he might have needed. The usual feeling that such borrowing was undesirable influenced him very strongly, however, and he refused to accept the offer.

An Unwise Policy

I felt at the time, and still feel, that the policy of my friend was not wise. He was satisfying the dictates of his conscience, it is true, but he was losing out every day on opportunities which could easily have been his and which would never come to him again. A loan of $300 annually after the first year would have placed him comparatively on "easy street." It would have given him twelve or fifteen hours a week for things other than outside work. The advantage of fraternity life, of societies, of training in certain activities, and of the thousand and one other opportunities of college life to obtain breadth and enjoyment might all have been his. Like so many others under similar circumstances, he was too busy earning money to perceive what he was missing. ·

Borrowing Too Much

A contrasting case is that of a man who attended a preparatory school for two years and an expensive technical institution for four, all on borrowed funds. At the time of his graduation from the technical school the entire amount of his indebtedness was more than $5,500. Needless to say this man, handicapped with such a debt, soon found himself facing a serious situation. The table shown in Figure 5, based upon the income of an average technical graduate and the estimated expenses of the man in question, shows that for the first few years still more money must be borrowed, in order to sustain the interest payments on this debt. According to the estimates, the full amount of the loan could not be paid off until fifteen years after graduation.

Students or parents borrowing funds for educational purposes should be able to determine the number of years it will take after graduation to repay the amount of their indebtedness. By following the directions given below similar calculations can be made for any case. The value of such a table lies, not so much in the possibility of its being followed exactly, as in showing the borrower approximately where he stands.

	1	2	3	4	5	6	7	8	9
Payment of $5500 Loan after Graduation									
Year	Probable Earnings	Living Expenses	Insurance Payments	Amount of Loan	Interest	Total Income	Total Expenses	Deposit Withdrawal	Bank Balance
				5500.					1100.
1 1933	1000.	1000.	91.	6600.	396	1000.	1487.	-487.	613.
2 34	1200.	1100.	91.	"	396	1200.	1557	-357.	226.
3 35	1500.	1200.	91.	"	396	1500.	1657.	-157.	59.
4 36	1800.	1200.	91.	"	396	1800.	1657.	+113.	152.
5 37	2000.	1300.	91.	"	396	2000.	1757.	+213.	365.
6 38	2300.	1400.	193.	"	396	2300.	1957.	+311.	776.
7 39	2600.	1500.	193.	"	396	2600.	2087.	+511.	1289.
8 40	2900.	1900.	193.	5600.	336	2900.	2429.	-529.	760.
9 41	3200.	2200.	193.	"	336	3200.	2729.	+471.	1231.
10 42	3500.	2400.	193.	4600.	276	3500.	2869.	-366.	862.
11 43	3500.	2400.	300.	3600.	216	3500.	2916.	-116.	746.
12 44	4000.	2500.	300.	2600.	156	4000.	2956.	+44.	790.
13 45	4300.	2500.	300.	1600.	96	4300.	2896.	+504.	1294.
14 46	4500.	2600	300.	—	—	4500.	2900.	—	1294.
15 47	5000	2600.	300.		96.	5096.	2900.	+2196	3490.

Figure 5. Table Showing Time Taken to Repay Loan

Directions for Computing Payment of Loan

1. The probable earnings are first filled in for as many years as necessary.

2. The probable living expenses are next inserted, as is also the amount of insurance payments for each year.

3.   The amount of the present indebtedness is placed in the column headed "Amount of Loan."

4.   The interest to be paid on the loan for one year is then calculated and placed in the column headed "Interest."

5.   The figures for the "Totals" columns are filled in for the first year. The total income is the earnings plus any other receipts. The total expense is living expense plus the payments on insurance, interest, etc.

6.   The necessary increase or possible decrease of the loan for the following year is then calculated and this amount recorded in the column headed "Deposits and Withdrawals."

7.   Steps (1) and (2) are then repeated for the following year, and the new amount of the loan is filled in as noted under (3). The calculations may be continued in the same manner indefinitely until the year is reached, when all indebtedness is removed. The capital necessary to carry the loan is shown as a bank balance. While this money, if actually on hand, should be reinvested to yield from 4 to 6 per cent interest, the accuracy of the other estimates does not warrant adding these interest payments to the income.

Earning Money in College

There is one advantage of earning money in college which cannot well be overlooked. This is the fact that men who earn all or part of their living and collegiate expenses are continually impressed with the cost of their education to them, in terms of their own services. This almost inevitably has the effect of making a man anxious to get the most out of what he receives.

It might be safe to say that every man would appreciate more the value of an education if he were made to earn each year a part of the money required to pay his expenses. It is equally safe to add that under ordinary circumstances a man makes a mistake in trying to earn any very large percentage of this money during the school year. A man in college or technical school who cannot make his time while there more valuable than 50 cents or $1 an hour, ought to find his occupation elsewhere.

There are rare cases where a man will be so well repaid either in money or experience gained that he will actually be well repaid for giving up a considerable amount of his time to outside work. I have in mind the case of a man in a small eastern college who managed the school bookstore for three years. In addition to the salary and commissions, which together amounted to about $600 during the year, this position gave an excellent opportunity for experience in selling and in many other phases of business. A comparatively small amount of time was spent, and the wages received averaged over $2 an hour.

Men who can develop special talent, such as

musical ability, fall into the same category. Tutoring also offers special opportunities, since it can be made to yield returns in valuable experience and training as well as in substantial remuneration. Such occupations, when they yield especially attractive compensation, may actually be worth while.

In most institutions, however, there are few such opportunities, and the most that can be squeezed from outside work is between 35 and 60 cents an hour. It is difficult on this basis to make earnings amount to more than $9 to $11 a week. In general, there are too many other things in which time can and should be well invested—such as friends, activities, and studies—to make the "odd job" pay.

Summary—A One-Year Program

In summing up the methods of making the two ends meet, we find first that a student pressed for funds should watch with special care his standing in his studies. By doing this he will be better able not only to win a possible scholarship, but also to complete his course in the allotted time. The second best means of obtaining money is to borrow, but this should be done only up to a conservative amount. Great care should be taken to maintain personal credit by prompt payments of interest and principal. And finally, earning money during the school year, while it has certain advantageous effects, may be considered on the whole to be a doubtful policy, especially when carried to the extreme.

No matter how carefully students and parents may analyze the facts and conditions, there will always be those who are uncertain as to whether the resources available are adequate. The requirements of a technical school, especially, cannot be considered easy to meet. When doubt exists the trial and error method is one of the best to apply.

A student who can put himself through his first year, unhampered by financial difficulties, on his own resources and those of his parents, should do so. Every effort should be made to free him from the necessity of working or of securing additional funds during the year. When this is done the chances for both immediate and final success are greatly improved. After one year, or better still two years, have been completed successfully, it is far easier to approach an outsider for assistance in order to complete the course. Even though apparent failure should result, maximum benefits will be derived from what will, in the long run, prove to be a minimum expenditure of time and money.

CHAPTER XIV

PERSONAL FINANCES AND EXPENSE ACCOUNTS[1]

The sooner you adjust your spending to what your earning capacity will be, the easier they will find it to live together.—"LETTERS FROM A SELF-MADE MERCHANT TO HIS SON."

Why Keep an Expense Account?

It very often happens that a student will go to considerable trouble to keep an expense account without apparently any definite reasons for doing so—unless it is by order of his parents! Not long ago I was talking with a man who had just completed his freshman year in a technical school. He had kept a careful expense account throughout the year, yet he admitted he did not know why he had done so. There are some very good reasons for keeping an account of your expenses, and they are well worth keeping in mind.

Budgeting Your Expenses

A very good reason why you should keep an expense account is to help you to plan or "budget" your finances. Many students whose money

---

[1] In compiling this chapter the author is indebted to Messrs. E. G. Plowman, J. B. Baker, and Professor M. J. Shugrue of the Economics Department of the Massachusetts Institute of Technology, and to Mr. H. B. McIntyre, Class of 1922, and Professor E. E. Bugbee, Department of Mining.

comes from home run short of cash several times during a term. This is because they do not look ahead in the matter of finances. It is just as important to plan your finances as to plan your time, your energy, or your work.

In business, financial planning is done by means of a budget. A good personal expense account serves as an individual budget. It will help you to adopt businesslike methods in handling your finances and by its aid you can plan your income, your expenditures, and your savings in advance.

Satisfaction from Businesslike Methods

A second benefit which comes from handling your personal finances in a businesslike manner is the personal satisfaction to be derived. This feeling of satisfaction will appeal more strongly to some than to others, but it is something which may well be cultivated. The greater advance you make in handling your financial affairs in an efficient, businesslike manner, the greater the enjoyment you will derive.

Practical Value of Knowing How to Keep Accounts

It is quite possible to learn much regarding accounting methods from your bookkeeping system. A professor at the Massachusetts Institute of Technology, who had formerly been employed as manager of a small mine, told me of his first experience as assistant to the treasurer of the company. For several years he had kept a simple set of books for his personal accounts. Shortly after he began work with the company the treasurer died. In the emergency the new assistant was called to take over the company's books and bring them up to date. His training as a mining engineer gave him little help. It was only through the knowledge gained with his own personal accounts, and by relying upon the assumption that all necessary transactions must have been recorded on the books at least once before, that he was able to carry the work along. Later he became the acting treasurer, and before leaving the company's employ, general manager.

No matter what sort of specialist you may plan to be, you will also need to know something about the handling of money. There is scarcely an easier or more profitable way of learning this than to keep an accurate account of your own personal finances.

Employer's Point of View

Some employers, moreover, place great emphasis upon the keeping of personal accounts.

If you are ever quizzed in regard to this when applying for a position you will discover that there is a vast difference between the good and the bad impression which one can make on this point. The reason why employers regard accuracy in keeping personal finances as important is obvious. If a position is one in which a man will be called upon to keep in order certain affairs of the company, the employer knows that he is better suited to do this if he has learned how to take care of his own affairs. The man who handles his personal finances in a slip-shod manner is likely to handle the company's business in the same way. It pays to be careful about "little things."

Learning to Save in College

A final reason for keeping an expense account is to learn to be thrifty and to save money. Few realize the full significance of acquiring these habits early, but the truth is that if these habits are not acquired early in life they are not likely to be acquired at all. By the time a man has completed his college course he should have learned the knack of saving a portion of his income.

The amount which you save is not so important. The question is whether or not you are putting aside any money out of that which you receive. If, by careful planning and wise spending, you can save 10 cents each day you will have $25.50 at the end of the school year (35 weeks) or more than enough ordinarily to pay your doctor's and dentist's bills, or to buy shoes and a couple of hats. Twenty cents a day is not a great amount to save, yet if you will set this aside each day during your eight years of high school and college, and allow the interest to be compounded at 4 per cent semiannually, you will find a fund amounting to over $700 available at the time you graduate.

There is no time like the present to begin putting aside a few cents each day. The right kind of expense account is often the best possible aid in doing this.

Choosing an Accounting Method to Meet Your Needs

Whether you are in high school, preparatory school, or college, an accounting method can be devised which will fit your particular needs. In some cases the best system may be extremely simple. In fact, it should never be more complex than absolutely necessary. It is often the case, however, that the more advanced methods of keeping accounts appear complicated at first sight, while in reality they can be maintained more easily and with less expenditure of time than the cruder methods.

Eventually you will want to develop for your personal finances a suitable accounting system. This will include a method of financial control over daily expenditures, together with a series of accounts to handle savings, borrowed money, etc. To develop such a system requires considerable experience. It is essential that you begin with the simpler methods described.

For the man who is just beginning to struggle with the problems of personal finance, the simple journal entry method or the columnar expense account is the only one that should be attempted at the start. Read over all the descriptions of accounting methods in this chapter before deciding to adopt any particular plan.

The Simplest Cash Account—The Record Journal

The simplest way of recording expenditures is by means of a simple journal. This consists of a suitable form, either in a notebook or book or a pocket fold, which provides for filling in the date, a description of each transaction, and the amounts of cash received or expended. A sample of a simple journal record is shown in Figure 6.

		Month of January 192-					
Jan	1	Brought Fwd		4	53		
		Breakfast					30
		Check Cashed No 51		10			
		Paper, ink, etc.				1	43
		Lunch					55
		Carfare					20
		Shoes				7	50
Jan	31	Carfare					10
		Dinner					65
		Totals		102	45	97	26
		Balance				5	19*
				5	19*		
		*Should check with cash on hand					

Figure 6. Simple Journal Cash Record

The advantages of such an account are:

1.   It is simple and easily understood.

2.   It gives full details regarding all expenditures made.

3.   It may be balanced as frequently or as infrequently as desired.

The disadvantages of such an account are:

1.   It does not furnish any information in regard to the proportion of money spent in various ways, as, for example, the relative amounts spent on clothing, rent, food, etc,

2.   It gives no knowledge concerning the financial status except that it shows the amount of cash on hand.   Bank accounts or other assets or liabilities are not shown.

3.   Entries must be made when the cash is actually received or expended in order to insure accurate records.   This is often inconvenient and impracticable.

4.   If the account is infrequently balanced the liability of error is great.

Analyzing Your Expenditures

After a simple journal record has been carefully kept for a time, the desirability of making an analysis of expenditures usually becomes apparent.   Certain items, such as those for school supplies, room rent, transportation, etc., appear to fall readily into separate groups, and to warrant segregation from other classes of expenditures. It is not well to carry the classification too far at first. A simple analysis should be made at the start, which later can be subdivided if necessary. Such a classification of expenditures, applicable to practically any student, might be as follows:

Educational Expense
Living Expense
Recreational and Miscellaneous Expenses

The Columnar Expense Account

The simplest way to obtain an analysis of your personal expenditures is probably by means of the columnar expense account. It is not necessary to describe here this plan in detail, since any number of small columnar account books on the market outline it very clearly. In general the columus in such a book, taken from left to right across the page, give space for the date, cash receipts, remarks, the amount of cash disbursed under each subdivision of expense, and the total expenditures for the day. At the bottom of each page space should be provided for totaling the various columns, and for checking the account at the end of the month.

One of the primary purposes of a columnar expense account is to furnish a record of the way in which money has been spent. In case it is desired to send such information home, for example, the complete account book, or the loose leaf of a notebook on which the record has been kept, can be sent through the mail very readily. If the record is not of the loose-leaf type, it is simply necessary to purchase a similar book to use for the following month, while the first set of records is being inspected and returned.

Briefly, the advantages of the columnar account are:

1. It can be operated by practically any student without the aid of special knowledge or equipment.

2. It gives a fairly complete record of how money is spent, with an analysis of expenditures as detailed as desired.

The disadvantages of columnar accounts are:

1. It gives no great incentive for saving and does not provide reserves.

2. It is not sufficient for handling all the problems which arise in connection with personal finances, as, for example, for giving information in regard to savings and money borrowed.

3. In order to obtain information regarding proportional expenditures, monthly computations must be made.

4. It must be kept without fail from day to day.

Standardizing Expenditure and Income

After having been away at school or college a year or two, you will probably find that your expenditures are made with fair regularity.

That is, over the period of a year they pass through approximately the same changes, and for corresponding months they are very similar. You will have learned also that over a considerable period of time, such as six months, a certain per cent of your income is spent on each of a regular set of items. By the time expenditures have become standardized to this extent you will probably also be receiving a regular income.

Your next step is then to learn how to set aside reserves for the regular expenditures and for many of the irregular ones which occur, and thus to place your finances on a more businesslike basis. This problem which you face is almost identical to the one you will encounter in after life. The sooner you prepare to meet such requirements the better.

A Financial Control Sheet[2]

One of the best, simplest, and most effective methods of accomplishing the desired results is by means of a financial control sheet. This method, after one has become familiar with its principles, is actually easier to operate than is the columnar account. Though not so accurate

---

[2] A detailed description of a Financial Control Sheet has been copyrighted by Professor Erwin H. Schell of the Massachusetts Institute of Technology. Parts of this are used here by permission.

in detail as the latter, its results are on the whole more satisfactory.

When properly laid out and operated, the financial control sheet achieves the following aims:

1. It gives you, in a simple, practical manner, facts concerning your financial condition at the end of each day.

2. It provides you with reserve funds for meeting oncoming obligations.

3. It gives you opportunity to set standards of daily savings and expenditures and provide information concerning your success or failure in maintaining these standards.

4. It develops an incentive to spend wisely and with foresight.

Developing a Financial Control Sheet

The first step in making out a financial control sheet is to purchase a pad, or better still a suitable book, of columnar-ruled paper, having from eleven to sixteen columns to the sheet, with a space at the left-hand edge for titles. Such paper is extensively used by accountants and may be obtained at most stationery stores.

After you have furnished yourself with the necessary materials (a slide rule at hand may prove useful) you are ready to lay out your control sheet. Do this first in pencil, as many changes will likely be necessary during the first month or two. Enter in the left-hand space titles which describe the subdivisions of income and expenditures. At first make these similar to the items shown in Figure 7. After running the sheet for a week or so you will know better what changes to make.

Number the columns on the sheet to correspond to the days of the month. Then spread all items, such as "Accruing Allowance," "Room Rent," "Savings," "Reserves," etc., across the sheet, as shown in the sample. Read over very carefully the detailed description of the sample financial control sheet shown (see page 164) before attempting a plan of your own, in order that you may understand fully the principles and methods involved.

Description of a Sample Control Sheet

The financial control sheet is divided into two distinct parts. The upper section of the sheet, headed "Incoming," lists those items of income which are accruing to the credit of the individual. The lower section, headed "Outgoing," lists the items such as "Board and Room," which are accruing against the individual, and which sooner or later must be paid. In the lower section also are being set aside certain reserves, such as

"Week-ends and Entertainment," which will be reduced as money is expended for items coming under this head.

An important point to notice on the sample sheet is that the amount of $4 just to the right of "Accruing Allowance," which represents the allowance accruing daily as income, is equal to the sum of the daily outgoing amounts. ($4 = $2 + .30 + .30 + .10 + .80 + .20 + .30.) A similar equation should be worked out as a basis for any control sheet. The use of round numbers, as in the above sample, obviates the use of a slide rule, but may require slight adjustments at the end of the month. It is advisable to spread as many of the allowances and reserves as possible across the page at the beginning of each period, in order to reduce the chance of error.

A detailed description of the transactions recorded on the sample sheet is as follows:

Thursday, April 1, Incoming. The allowance for April has evidently not been received. The amount of $120 is due, and appears opposite "Accruing Allowance" (together with the $4 accrued for the first day). The figures opposite "Cash on Hand," "Check Account," and "Due from others," are self-explanatory.

Outgoing. The room rent is not yet paid ($60); there has been a reserve built up for laundry and clothing amounting to $5.30; for week-ends, etc., $3.20; for church, etc., $2.40; and for a typewriter, $29.80. There is only a 20-cent reserve for miscellaneous items. The savings to date have amounted to $12. One dollar is due to others.

Friday, April 2, Incoming and Outgoing. The allowance has evidently been received and deposited in the checking account at the bank. This would bring the bank balance up to $232.40, had not a check been drawn for $10, which increases the cash on hand. Part of the $10, however, was expended for laundry ($5.30 + .30 — $1.40 = $4.20). Ninety cents was also spent on miscellaneous items (lunch, candy, etc.). No expenditure was made which was not provided for in the reserves, so that the balance for the second day is the same as for the first, $133.03.

Saturday, April 3, Incoming and Outgoing. A check was evidently drawn for $60 to pay the board and room bill for the month. The week-end expenditures for this particular Saturday amounted to $4.80, so that the reserve for this item was reduced to minus $1, shown by drawing a circle around the figure ($3.50 + .30 — $4.80 = — $1). There was an understanding between the student and his parents that as soon as $30 had been reserved for a typewriter the remaining $20 would be forwarded. The check arrived as promised, and is shown as the last item of income, while the reserve for the typewriter is increased immediately to $50. It should also be noticed that the 20 cents which previously was being set aside each day for the typewriter reserve has now been distributed between "Laundry and Clothing" and "Miscellaneous."

Saturday, April 4, Incoming and Outgoing. A check for $30 was placed with the special check for $20 and

Financial Control Sheet				
Month of April	Thur.	Fri.	Sat.	Sun.
Incoming				
Receiving Allowance $4.00	124.-	8.-	12.-	16.-
Cash on hand	6.53	14.25	8.55	11.75
Check Account	112.40	222.40	162.40	132.40
Due from others	6.-	6.-	6.-	—
Special Funds	Check for Typewriter 20.-			
Total	248.93	250.65	208.95	160.15
Outgoing				
Board & Room $2.00	62.-	64.-	6.-	6.-
Laundry & Clothing 30¢	5.30	4.20	4.60	5.-
Weekends & Entertainment 30¢	3.20	3.50	(1.00)	(.70)
Church, etc. 10¢	2.40	2.50	2.60	1.70
Miscellaneous 80¢	.20	.10	.15	2.5
Reserve (Typewriter) 20¢	29.50	30.-	50.-	—
Savings 30¢	12.-	12.30	12.60	12.90
Due others	1.-	1.-	1.-	—
Total	115.90	117.60	75.95	27.75
Balance	133.03	133.05	133.03	133.03

Figure 7.   Financial Control Sheet

a typewriter was ordered. The $6 due from others was received, and the $1 owed was paid. One dollar was given to church and 80 cents was spent on miscellaneous items. This completed the transactions for the day. The final balance is seen to have remained the same throughout.

Once the control sheet is established and the standard for expenditures is set, the important figures to watch are the Balance and the Reserves. If these are approximately the same at the end of the month as at the beginning it is evident that the income is equal to the expenditures and that the proper apportionment of expenses has been made. If any reserve grows too large during the month the daily allotment to that item should be reduced, and the amount thus made available should be then allotted to some decreasing reserve item, or to a "Savings Reserve."

At the first of each month, when a new sheet is begun, a reasonable amount should be set down for each reserve. If the balance when struck is then too large, some of the money together with any "Savings Reserve" may be withdrawn from the checking account and deposited elsewhere as savings. If the balance tends to become smaller each month, more funds must be supplied in order to make up the deficit.

Advantages and Disadvantages

Summarizing the advantages and disadvantages of the financial plan outlined above, they are seen to be as follows:

ADVANTAGES:

1. It gives an excellent idea of the proportions in which money is spent for various items without the need of monthly recapitulations. In the example shown, for instance, it is evident at a glance that approximately 7½ per cent of the total income (.30 ÷ $4) is being spent for laundry and clothing, and the same proportion is also being set aside for week-ends and entertainments and for savings.

2. It furnishes a strong incentive to make expenditures wisely and with forethought, and to save a certain per cent of the income.

3. There is not the absolute necessity of making entries on the sheet each day without fail. Failure to calculate the reserves and balance for one or more days omits the information which these figures would give, but does not cause undue confusion in calculations which follow. Not more than five or ten minutes is required each night for making all necessary entries and calculations.

DISADVANTAGES:

1. In order to use the financial control sheet to best advantage one should be able to anticipate a certain regularity of income and expense.

2. It requires some time to become familiar with this method. A certain amount of time (approxi-

mately ½ hour) is also required at the beginning of each month to reapportion the reserves and to spread the items over the sheet for the month following.

3. Familiarity with the use of the slide rule, so that the latter may be used in calculating the daily accruing income and expenditures, is desirable, though not absolutely necessary.

Double-Entry Accounting

As already stated, it is well for any student to adopt sooner or later methods of business accounting in handling at least a part of his personal financial problems. Nevertheless, it is unwise to strike out blindly here, since many difficulties may be encountered which are confusing to a beginner.

As a student in college or technical school you should determine to gain a knowledge of the principles of accounting as soon as possible. This you may do by taking either a regular course or a correspondence school course in accounting. The subject matter is such that many find it very difficult to learn accounting practice from the study of books alone.

Do not attempt to install any features of double-entry accounting in your personal accounts until you have become familiar with the underlying principles involved. On the other hand, once you have gained a knowledge of accounting methods, you will find no better way of clinching your knowledge than by applying it to your own personal accounts. The use of some of the books listed in the bibliography at the end of this chapter, together with instructions or suggestions from men familiar with such practice in business, will prove of assistance in getting started on this work.

Simple Double-Entry Accounts

The operation of double-entry accounts can be shown very well in connection with the permanent maintenance of a financial control sheet or other personal accounting record. The most satisfactory means of combining the control method with a set of ledger accounts requires the use of two adjustment or intermediate accounts. These may be termed the "Allotment Account" and the "Control Sheet Account." At first sight the correlation by this means may appear cumbersome. In reality, further simplification causes confusion, while the maintaining of two accounts adds nothing to the work of keeping the books. Examples of an Investment Account and the two other accounts mentioned are shown in Figures 8, 9, and 10. The method of using these in conjunction with a financial control sheet, or other personal cash accounting system, is also described.

The entries in the above accounts are explained as follows:

On October 1, $5 was allotted from the control sheet to the Investment Account. This is shown by the credit (right-hand) entry on the Allotment Account,

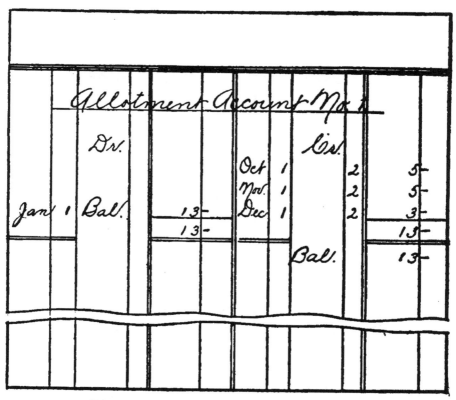

Figure 8.   An Allotment Account

and the debit (left-hand) entry on the Control Sheet Account.

On November 1, the $5 allotted was paid from the control sheet into the investment fund. This is shown by the credit entry on Account No. 2 and the debit on No. 3.

On November 1 also it was decided again to allot $5 to be withdrawn from the spending money at the end of the month. This is shown as before by a credit entry on No. 1 and a debit on No. 2.

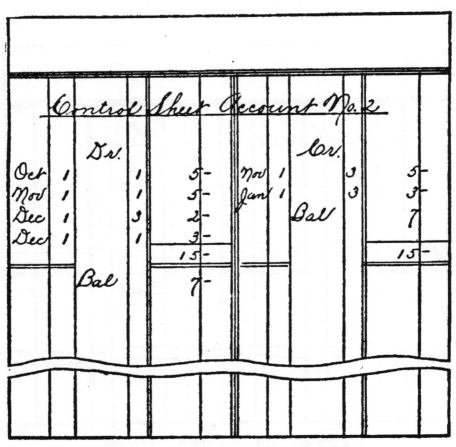

Figure 9. A Control Sheet Account

During the month of November, however, larger cash expenditures were evidently made than were anticipated. The final balance on the control sheet was therefore decreased, and instead of putting money into the Investment Account it was necessary to withdraw $2. This is shown by the debit entry on No. 2 and the credit entry on No. 3.

Since savings were not made as rapidly as antici-pated it was further decided to allot only $3 to be turned over to the Investment Account for the month

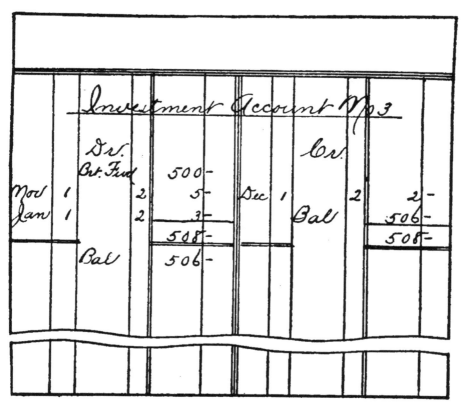

Figure 10. An Investment Account

of November. This shows on the accounts as a credit to No. 1 and debit to No. 2.

On January 1, $3 was transferred from the control sheet to the investment fund (No. 2 credit, No. 3 debit) and balances were struck. The following facts are immediately evident:

1. $13 has been allotted to be saved out of the personal expenses fund during the three months noted. (See balance of Allotment Account.)

2.   Out of the $13 allotted the control sheet has still to pay over $7 to the investment fund.   (Balance of No. 2.)   Hence $6 has actually been "saved" during the months of October, November, and December ($13 — $7 = $6).

3.   The balance in the Investment Account has been increased from $500 on November 1 to $506 on January 1, which checks with the above statement that $6 has actually been turned into the investment fund as savings.

It should be noted that in case it is necessary to continually reimburse the control sheet from the investment fund allotments can be made (debit No. 1, credit No. 2) which will anticipate such payments.   This method of recording transactions is sufficiently elastic, therefore, to take care of practically any conditions which may arise.

Outline of a Practical Double-Entry System

It is clear that by the above method a permanent relationship can be established between a financial control sheet, or any other method of recording personal cash expenditures, and a series of ledger accounts.   Each month money may be allotted from a savings account to the control sheet, for example, or vice versa.   If this allotment is not maintained the actual status will be shown clearly and simply by the monthly balances. Hence with such an arrangement there will be a double force tending toward economical spending. Savings are not only pushed into the Investment Account by the operations of the control sheet, but are also drawn into the same account by the entries made under "Allotment."

A little reflection will show that this method represents in simple form an elastic system of handling personal finances which is widely applicable. The Investment Account may, in fact, be broken down into any number of asset and liability accounts. The advantages are gained by using double-entry accounting where it is necessary, and the disadvantages of recording small daily expenditures by this means are avoided.

BIBLIOGRAPHY

Beach, F. L. Twenty Twenty-Minute Lessons in Bookkeeping.

Cole, W. M. Fundamentals of Accounting.

Hodge, A. C., and McKinsey, J. O. Principles of Accounting.

Koopman, S. B., and Kester, R. B. Fundamentals of Accounting.

Paton, W. A., and Stevenson, R. A. Principles of Accounting.

CHAPTER XV

SUMMER WORK, GETTING A JOB AND MAKING GOOD

When a man does not know to what port he is steering no wind is favorable to him.—SENECA

A Definite Aim

It is important that as a student in college or a technical school you should formulate for yourself as early as possible a definite purpose in life. The problem of knowing just what you want to do is a difficult one to solve. The earlier you are able to describe clearly some goal toward which you are striving, the better.

The importance of making an early choice can be shown in a number of ways. At Dartmouth comparative records have recently been compiled of the students who had early chosen their life work and those who had not. The scholastic standing of the former appeared to be 5 or 6 per cent higher than that of those who were simply drifting. There was shown also a better correlation between studies, outside work, and other activities. This was especially true in the selection of general studies. By setting a goal for yourself you have a double advantage. Not only does it give you something definite toward which to strive, but also it helps you to select and shape your experiences in such a way that they will fit more perfectly into your scheme of life as a whole. Even if you do not stick to the exact profession for which you train yourself, you will be much farther ahead at the end of ten years for having had a definite purpose in mind while in college.

Summer Work and Choosing a Profession

It is generally supposed that men taking technical courses have definitely settled upon a professional career. In reality this is rarely true. Many technical students have a clearer conception of their future work than do college men. Nevertheless, these aims are often very vague. It is shown by the records of graduates that men trained for special service in particular fields of engineering often find their vocation elsewhere.[1]

There is a close relationship between choosing a profession and experience gained through summer work. During the past year a part of my work with seniors has been to attempt to connect their past experiences with their plans for the future. Some of these men had done little sum-

---

[1] It is doubtful if more than 15 per cent of all technical graduates remain in what might be considered to be strictly technical fields for longer than 7 or 8 years after graduation.

mer work during their four years' course. The
majority had gained practical experience in one
way or another during at least two summers, and
showed excellent records. For example, one man
had worked for six summers in six automobile
plants.

A most striking fact was correlation between
the amount of summer work and definiteness in
regard to future plans. Not one of the men who
had done no summer work during his years of
training had any clear conception of what he expected to do after graduation.

Specific Gains Through Summer Experience

Experience in industry, besides intermixing
practice with theory, gives a student a background for a reliable study of his own abilities
and limitations. A man cannot be expected to
know whether he will find the profession of a
boiler expert to his liking until he has a taste of
the required work.

Engineering schools are realizing more and
more clearly the value of practical experience obtained in conjunction with technical courses. Statistics from ten representative institutions indicate that in the year 1921-1922 there were between three and four times as many men taking
co-operative technical courses as there had been

eight years previous, while the number of regular students during this period had increased only some 33 1/3 per cent. It is evident that steps are being taken by schools themselves to require practical training as a part of every technical course. If this has not been done in your school, your policy may well be to gain this experience through your own initiative.

Obtaining Proper Experience

The training to be gained during summers and after graduation should be selected upon a long-term basis, for this determines your experience to a great extent. A short time ago I discussed this subject with a man who has carried on an increasingly successful business for over thirty years. "Let your plans be laid with a view to succeeding when success counts the most," he said. "It does not matter so much what you will do when you are five years out of school. It is what you will be doing after you have been out ten years or more that counts. Succeed if you can before you are thirty, but let your success be of that kind which leads on to greater achievements when you are more than forty."

Before you can be truly successful in the broadest sense, there are at least three things which you must acquire by experience: You must know how to control men; you must be able to gain the confidence of your employers and co-workers; and you must be able to sell your product, whether that product is your own services or manufactured goods. To achieve these ends practical experience, as well as natural aptitude and acquired knowledge, is demanded.

Suggestions for Summer Work

Below is an analysis of the various types of summer work open to students. If carefully studied this section should aid you in deciding what kind of work will give the needed experience.

ENGINEERING EXPERIENCE AND TECHNICAL WORK

In this field may be included all work of a fairly technical nature which does not include the learning of a particular trade. Such, for example, would be:

Designing and drafting
Surveying
Constructive work
Research work (industrial or professional)

TRADE OCCUPATIONS

These include all jobs related directly to specific trades. The great value of experience gained here lies in obtaining the point of view of the workingman, as well as in learning the details of certain tasks through actual performance. Examples:

Machine shop work
Foundry work

Forging
Electrician's work
Wood turning

GENERAL INDUSTRIAL EXPERIENCE

By this is meant training of a relatively broad nature in industrial plants. Such work should give every opportunity for studying the various processes and methods employed in modern manufacturing. It can usually be found best in the departments of:

Purchasing
Storing
Shipping
Receiving
General office work (under certain conditions)

STATISTICAL AND ACCOUNTING EXPERIENCE

This includes work in the accounting department or in statistical departments of industrial plants, as well as in banks, brokerage houses, accountants' offices, etc. The experience is very valuable in teaching the methods of recording and to some extent of financing used in business.

SALES EXPERIENCE

Certain types of selling are essential in practically every field. Training in this work, even for the man who does not intend to use the experience directly, is very valuable. An analysis of various kinds of sales occupations might include:

Mail order work
Selling goods to other firms
Selling goods to individuals (house-to-house canvassing, etc.)
Advertising work

Work for Financial Returns
    Tutoring
    Summer camp counsellor work
    Work as chauffeur
    Running motor boat
    Operating wireless, etc.
    Hotel service

Suggested Programs

General recommendations as to what sort of summer experiences is most desirable are difficult to make; individual cases require special treatment. The programs given below, however, have actually been followed by many men. The suggestions they contain are based upon the experiences of students well satisfied with the results obtained, and upon the recommendations of older men who have observed these results. All programs, of course, are subject to revision in cases where men must carry special courses or do other required work during any particular summer.

For the man who leans by choice to strictly technical training and who feels that a professioual field has a special appeal, a plan similar to the following is good:

Summer after First Year
Surveying or other outdoor work.
Industrial experience of a general nature.

If absolutely necessary work giving the greatest possible remuneration rather than the most valuable experience.

SUMMER AFTER SECOND YEAR
Trade occupation.

SUMMER AFTER THIRD YEAR
Trade occupation.
Construction work.

If, on the other hand, you are a student who feels more inclined to enter into some particular industry or business, your program might be laid out as follows:

SUMMER AFTER FIRST YEAR
Selling experience.
Trade occupation.

SUMMER AFTER SECOND YEAR
Selling experience. (Stick to it until you are successful.)
Industrial experience of a general nature.
Trade occupation, if not taken the first summer.

SUMMER AFTER THIRD YEAR
Industrial experience.
Statistical or accounting experience.

Still another plan may be followed by students who desire to go into research work. For such men a program might be laid out as follows:

SUMMER AFTER FIRST YEAR
Work of a general industrial nature, in connection with a research department if possible.
Work for financial returns if this is a necessity.

SUMMER AFTER SECOND YEAR
Industrial research work of a general character.

SUMMER AFTER THIRD YEAR
Somewhat more highly specialized work in professional or industrial research.

Getting the Job

The procedure of actually obtaining the position you want is even more a matter of individual
initiative, judgment, and energy. A few books
have recently appeared which will be well worth
your while to consult in this connection.[2] According to these books, and according to the experience of a number of students, the following
points may be emphasized:

Planning Your Campaign

Do not trust to chance, or to a burst of last-
minute energy, but plan out your campaign in
advance, both as to the line of work you desire
and, so far as you can, the possible employer. If
you are going to line up a summer job for the latter part of June, for example, begin laying your
plans in March. Before you do anything else de-

---

[2] Two excellent books on the subject of getting a job which apply
very well to the undergraduate or to recent graduates are: "How to
Get the Job You Want," by William L. Fletcher, and "Finding Your
Job," by Norman G. Shidle. Mr. Fletcher is a man of wide employment experience and is well qualified to handle this subject in all its
aspects. Mr. Shidle is a more recent graduate and presents his material in a manner especially valuable to the young college or technical
student.

termine the kind of position you want to get—
and know *why* you want it. Make a memorandum of this. Have one or two alternatives if
you wish, but decide definitely on what kind of
work will be most desirable.

Obtain a good list of prospective employers.
To do this utilize fully the following possible
sources of information and assistance:

> Relatives and friends; business men and social
> acquaintances.
>
> Former teachers and teachers in your present
> school.
>
> Former employers.
>
> Graduates of your school and others especially
> interested, such as co-operating manufac-
> turers, etc.
>
> Industrial research divisions (school employ-
> ment departments).
>
> Commercial employment agencies of the
> Y. M. C. A.
>
> Engineering societies.
>
> Trade associations and United States govern-
> ment service.

Letters of Application

Very probably you will have to make your
contact with possible employers by letter. Make
your letters effective. Three essentials for a good
letter of application are:

1. It must contain the necessary facts.
2. The thoughts must be expressed in a logical, concise, and straightforward manner.
3. It must be mechanically perfect; that is, correct as to spacing, margins, spelling, neatness, and general appearance.

Before final typing be sure to have your letter scrutinized by the severest critic whom you can find. The typing should be done by an experienced stenographer on standard stationery. This will save you time and money in the end.

Below are shown two good letters of application:

32 Westland Ave.,
Boston, Mass.,
May 20, 1922.

Chain Belt Co.,
744 Park St.,
Milwaukee, Wis.

Gentlemen:

Inasmuch as I anticipate graduating in the course in Mechanical Engineering at the Massachusetts Institute of Technology (Boston Tech.) this coming June, I am taking the liberty of writing you with regard to possible openings in your concern at that time.

I am an American citizen, 28 years old. At the age of 16 I entered a machine shop in Washington, D. C., and served there eight years. During this period I attended trade and preparatory schools, completed my high school education, and attended evening sessions at George Washington University. While there I studied liberal arts and scientific subjects.

At the outbreak of the war I entered the first officers' training camp and was commissioned a 2nd Lieutenant in the Coast Artillery Corps. My service in the army covered a period of two years and four months, ten months of which were overseas. In August, 1919, I was honorably discharged as a 1st Lieutenant. The following September I entered this institution with advanced standing.

My practical experience includes also that gained during school vacations and covers a period of nine years spent in machine and forge shops at different manufacturing plants. Supplemented by school instruction, I have had liberal training in the operation of lathes, drill presses, milling machines and various other machine tools. At present I am a student assistant in the Machine Tool Laboratory. This, in itself, is an excellent training, as the laboratory is equipped with the lathes and most improved machine tools. My experience in drafting has been that gained in the army, three years at George Washington University, and three years at Technology.

The field in which I am directly interested is either Sales or Production Engineering. I realize that in order to prove of greatest value to a concern I must first occupy subordinate positions despite my previous training. This I am quite prepared to do.

With reference to my record and scholarship at the Institute I am able to refer you to Professor Edward F. Miller, head of the course in Mechanical Engineering.

Should you be interested, I should be pleased to forward any further information necessary, or arrange for an interview with any representative within a reasonable distance of Boston.

Very truly yours,

M. B. B.

Copies of this letter were sent to sixteen corporations. The writer received fifteen replies, four interviews, and three offers of positions. It will pay you to study this letter carefully. The style or tone of the letter is particularly worthy of your careful consideration.

81 Haddon Road,
Lexington, Massachusetts,
May 17, 1921.

Western Paper Manufacturing Company,
Springfield, Massachusetts.

Subject: Application for Position

Gentlemen:

I write to ask what opportunity your business can offer to a man 27 years of age with average ability, an open mind and a capacity for hard work. I write to you because I have had several years' experience in the paper industry, am interested in it above all other kinds of business and because I know your company by reputation to be the kind I should like to work with.

My education is high school and one year at Boston University (evenings), where I studied management and marketing problems. In the paper business I started at the bottom in a mill in Pennsylvania. When I entered the service in 1917 I was foreman of a department. Since the war I have had some experience in selling, printing, and buying—in other words, I have been trying to get an all-round knowledge before starting on the job which I shall try to make my life work.

There are personal qualities which have an important bearing upon a man's success—such as personality, loyalty, enthusiasm, reliability, resourcefulness and initiative—upon which I am not competent to speak regarding myself. I can say, however, that my health is excellent, I have a purpose in life, I can accept responsibilities, and I think that the army taught me the importance of discipline. I am saving a small amount of money regularly. As to character, habits and references, I can refer you to people with whom I have worked and invite such further investigation as you may care to make.

Because I am married and dependent upon what I earn for support I cannot afford to finance myself entirely during a trial period; initial salary, however, is a secondary consideration. What I desire is an opportunity to demonstrate my value to you. May I have the privilege of an interview at your convenience?

Sincerely yours,

Ernest Tuttle.

Persistence

Finally, and perhaps more important than any other advice that could be given: Be persistent. Stick to your campaign for a job until you get results.

BIBLIOGRAPHY

Barrett, C. R. Getting a Good Job.
Beveridge, A. J. Young Man and the World, The.
Bolwell, R. After College, What?
Cushing, G. H. Some Points to Remember When Looking for a Job.
Dibble, F. A. How to Get a Satisfactory Situation.
Fletcher, William L. How to Get the Job You Want.
Fowler, N. C., Jr. How to Get and Keep a Job.
Gowin, E. B. Occupations; A Textbook in Vocational Guidance.
Gunion, P. C. Selling Your Services.
Gurtler, F. H. Getting the Position.
Hendrick, Ellwood. Opportunities in Chemistry.
Hiscock, G. D. Modern Steam Engineering.
Horton, C. M. Opportunities in Engineering.
Lee, J. M. Opportunities in Newspaper Business.
Maxwell, William. If I Were Twenty-One.
Merton, H. W. How to Choose the Right Vocation.
Newell, F. H. Engineering as a Career.
Rollins, Frank West. What Can a Young Man Do?
Shidle, Norman G. Finding Your Job.

CHAPTER XVI

THE OTHER THINGS IN LIFE[1]

Till we are built like angels,
With hammer and chisel and pen
We will work for ourselves and a woman,
Forever and ever, amen.

—RUDYARD KIPLING

Girls and Their Proper Sphere

It will always be a question in the minds of parents, faculty, and students, whether or not girls play too large a part in a man's educational career. Whenever a man does poor work, or is on the verge of expulsion or flunking out, the age-old insinuation invariably comes up: "He dallied with women too much"!

It is part of a man's education to call upon and to go around with girls during his college course. The unfortunate type of man who is a recluse in this respect is very likely to regret that he has not taken advantage of his opportunities. If he has not adjusted his relationship with girls in a normal manner he is likely to fall into difficulties in after life. The man who does not understand women is likely to form unsuitable friendships,

---

[1] In writing this chapter the author is indebted to Mr. Henri Pell Junod, who collaborated with him in this work and in selecting quotations for the chapter headings throughout the book.

and eventually perhaps to find himself unhappily married. Moreover, women are the instinctive arbiters of social relations. Their influence in training men to adapt themselves to society is an almost indispensable factor. A man may be a technical genius but unless he knows something of social matters as well he will be doomed to many a business and financial defeat. The man who does not learn to get along with women while he is in college is neglecting an important lesson which should be mastered.

Overdoing the Matter

On the other hand there are many college men who rush headlong into the society game and become enveloped in a whirlpool of social activities, which culminates in their scholastic ruin. I recall the case of a friend who recently came to a technical school. He was interested in his fraternity, and in other activities which took a considerable portion of his time. Besides these, he insisted on attending all of the teas, dances, and theater parties to which he was invited. As a result he neglected his studies. Although he managed to "get by" for three years, in the middle of his senior year he was forced to drop out. All his trouble could easily have been avoided had he but exercised his better judgment.

There are four things to which every college man can devote his time; studies, fraternities, activities, and girls. A man has yet to be found who can undertake unlimited responsibilities in the last three and still carry on the first satisfactorily.

The Happy Medium

Aristotle said, "Medium courses are the best." As in the case of the ancients, each man must steer his course between his Scylla and Charybdis. Many indeed were destroyed between these two treacherous hazards, but a strong and firm Æneas piloted his vessel safely between them. There is a vast difference between going to see a girl or two during the week-end and going to a party every night.

A technical student must realize always that he has come to school, not necessarily to grind, but to work. He must deal with the "Girl Question" in a sensible manner. He cannot permit himself to acquire the habit of calling incessantly upon a girl, and must be content with being in such company a reasonable part of the time. Thus a man can obtain all the greatest benefits of society but at the same time he will not thwart his predominant purpose of gaining a technical training.

Week-Ends

Week-ends are likely to be the factor in the life of a student which actually make or break him. There are men who slave all day Sunday in order to make up back work. They are satisfied to make Saturday night and Sunday a veritable orgy of work, for they look on the week-end merely as a time to catch up in the work which they have neglected during the week. As a matter of fact, when it is time for bed Sunday night such men too often find that the week-end has been really frittered away and that only a few hours of constructive work have been accomplished .

There are, on the other hand, men who look upon Sunday as a day of absolute rest, but their rest too often consists of sleeping all the morning and sitting in an armchair during the remainder of the day. Possibly, to break the monotony they glance occasionally at "Boob McNutt," "Bringing up Father," or the "Sporting Section"!

The Problem

The problem of how to spend your week-ends profitably is a big one in itself. Moreover, the way in which you solve it now will influence you to solve it similarly throughout your life. No man wants to look forward to coming home Saturday noon when he has a home of his own, with the prospect of working incessantly till late Sunday night on "hang-over" work from the previous week. There is no time like the present to begin cultivating the habit of having your week's work done when the working week is over.

It was one of Roosevelt's ideals to fill every one of his week-ends with pastimes which were worth while. We can do no better than to follow in his footsteps. Between Saturday at 12 and Monday morning at 8 o'clock there are 44 hours available. Look upon these as a reward for your honest effort and the completion of your work during the week. Then follow Roosevelt's scheme, spending your time as you wish to spend it, but always to advantage.

Suggestions

Below are shown two types of week-ends. These are actual plans practiced by two friends over a period of four years.

I

Sat. P. M.	Ball game. Go to city (usually alone).
Sat. Night	Go to see family or friends.
Sun. A. M.	Church and Sunday School.
Sun. P. M.	Walk, see museums, etc. (usually alone).

| Sun. Night | Go to see friends. |
| | Go to bed early. |

2

Sat. P. M.	Track practice.
	Football game.
Sat. Night	Call on girls (with fellows).
Sun. A. M.	Read a newspaper or loaf.
Sun. P. M.	Talk with boys or play ball.
Sun. Night	Movies with fellows or girls.

The first of these week-ends is far too circumscribed; the man has accomplished a great deal but he has not broadened his relations with his fellows, and has been alone too much. The second man, although he has broadened his relations with his fellows, has entirely neglected the fact that he should try to improve his mind. Below is a third plan, by following which a man can avoid the dangers of both the first and second schemes above and at the same time can accomplish more and widen his outlook on life.

3

Sat. P. M.	Athletics, sports, or tootball game.
Sat. Night	Call upon girls.
Sun. A. M.	Read something worth while or go to church.

Sun. P. M.	Get some exercise.
Sun. Night	Help your friends.
	Write letters.
	Call upon a girl.
	See family and friends.
	Bed early.

Six Purposes of a Week-End

There are finally six purposes a man may well bear in mind when planning his week-ends. These are:

1. To improve his relations with his fellow men.
2. To improve his mind.
3. To meet and to get acquainted with girls.
4. To maintain perfect physical health.
5. To enjoy the association of family and home life.
6. To learn the lesson of helpfulness to others.

The man who can properly correlate in his week-ends these six points has indeed made a great advance toward ultimately gaining success and happiness in both his work and play.

Friends

Friendship is as old as the ages. It is the most sought-after blessing in the universe. It is elusive—yet elusive only in that men must give of themselves to obtain the fullness of it.

True friendship is not a superficial acquaintanceship; it is something deep and firmly founded in one's character. A friend is a man who knows all your faults—and likes you just the same. He is a man who will give you of his time, his money, his all; who is never too busy to help you or to advise you or to cheer you and who is willing to make your problems his own.

Tests of Friendship

The true test of friendship is adversity. This, indeed, proves the old saying, "A friend in need is a friend indeed." The spirit of sacrifice enters into every true friendship. No Damon-and-Pythias friendship, no David-and-Jonathan friendship, comes to the man who does not preach and practice the gospel of "give and take."

The friendships which one makes in life are among its rarest blessings. How truly has it been said that money and fame matter little as compared with friends and the happiness they can bring!

Obstacles

The greatest obstacle you will have to face in making friends is your own natural reticence. In college you must also remember that owing to inevitable conditions in the large institutions the custom of speaking and conversing freely with other men is far more limited than in smaller schools and colleges. It is only through your own initiative that you can overcome these difficulties.

Every day in the classroom, in activities, and after hours there are opportunities for you to make and cultivate friends. Do not let these chances escape you. Meet as many men as you can during your first year, for it is there that the roots of friendship first spring. After this you will find it increasingly easy to enjoy the company of men, and you will gain much from every new acquaintanceship.

Giving Yourself a Chance

In the world of competition you must realize that many men will do things well. Then when the problem comes of deciding between two men, whether it is a matter of letting a contract or obtaining a job or a raise in salary, if the ability of the two men is equal the question of friendship and capacity for making friends (which is nothing short of personality) usually decides the issue. It is worth everything to cultivate this ability and the time to begin is while you are in college. Today in business it is the man who makes friends first and does business afterwards who succeeds in the long run.

Attaining an Ideal

Friendship is an attainable ideal for everyone and it depends upon the individual to what extent he will put himself out to gain its full value. Like all else in life, it is governed by the principle that the more one puts into it the more one will get out.

Build your life upon your friendships. From your friends you will gain more happiness, more real enjoyment, more of the never-failing blessings of life than from any other single source of pleasure. Through them you will be able to render your greatest service. The man who builds up his life hopes, ambitions, and achievements upon a firm foundation of friendship can safely feel that his building is as secure as the great pyramids.

> True friendship is a Gordian Knot
> Which Angel hands have tied,
> By heavenly skill its texture wrought—
> Who shall its folds divide?